WILLIE THORNE

TAKING A PUNT ON MY LIFE

To Malcolm, Mum, Robert, Jill, Kieran, Tristan, Tahli,
Natalie and James.

WILLIE
THORNE

TAKING A PUNT ON MY LIFE

VSP

Published by Vision Sports Publishing in 2011

Vision Sports Publishing
19–23 High Street
Kingston upon Thames
Surrey
KT1 1LL

www.visionsp.co.uk

ISBN: 978-1-907637-17-9

Editor: Justyn Barnes
Copy editing: Alex Morton
Cover design: Doug Cheeseman
Cover photography: Clive Brunskill, Getty Images

Typeset by Palimpsest Book Production Limited,
Falkirk, Stirlingshire

Printed and bound by CPI Group (UK) Ltd, Croydon, CR0 4YY

A CIP Catalogue record for this book is
available from the British Library

CONTENTS

ACKNOWLEDGEMENTS

I would like to say thanks first and foremost to my family for their love and support, to my good friend John Hayes for his help and encouragement during the good times and the bad, to his son Matt and all at Champions UK, who are not only colleagues but friends as well.

My thanks go to Rick Mayson for helping to get this project off the ground, to Jim Drewett and Toby Trotman at Vision Sports Publishing for their belief in my story, and to Justyn Barnes for his editing skills. Finally I would like to thank Kevin Brennan who collaborated with me in writing this book, for his work in putting the whole thing together.

FOREWORD

By Dennis Taylor

I have known Willie for more years than either of us probably care to remember. One of the first trips we ever made together a very long time ago was to the Canadian Open. Things were a bit tight back then and we had to share a room. We got on really well and struck up a friendship that has remained to this day.

Over the years the two of us were always the ones who would go out for a meal and a chat in the evenings, or play golf if we had a day off when we were both playing in tournaments, and he was always very good company.

Willie was a very talented player and loved to attack when he was at the table. He was always looking to make big breaks, and perhaps that was something which stopped him winning more big tournaments than he did. He always played with a lot of class and was very quick around the table.

Willie and I were lucky to have been playing during a very good period for the game in the 1980s, and he very quickly became one of the sport's characters. I suppose we both had faces that stuck with the public, Willie with his bald head and moustache and me with my distinctive glasses. It made us recognisable to a wider audience, and I think our careers benefitted from that.

I remember once when we were playing in the Howard Keel Golf Classic, Willie and I went out for a drink in Manchester with the American actor John Ashton, who was very big at the time because he had appeared alongside Eddie Murphy in the *Beverley Hills Cop* trilogy of movies. All night people were coming up to Willie and I for a chat and autographs, while hardly noticing John. It just showed how popular snooker was in Britain at the time.

It was a different game back then, when playing exhibitions was one of your main sources of income. I used to crack a joke during exhibitions when I was setting up shots and there was no doubt that having a rapport with your audience was a big part of what you did.

Willie has always had that natural rapport with the fans, and they have always liked him because of it. He has admitted to having some difficult times with his gambling, and I am sure he would be the first to admit that his life would have been much easier if those problems had not been in the background for much of the time. I know that his wife Jill has also been a real gem in helping him come through some tough moments in his life.

Willie and I still see quite a bit of each other these days, and enjoy our time together whenever we share television commentating duties. Whenever we meet it isn't long before all the old stories re-surface once more and we're giggling like a couple of schoolboys. It's something I think we will always do and is a measure of the experiences we have shared together during all those years of playing snooker.

Willie is a lovely guy who has led a rich and colourful life. He has been one of snooker's great characters, and one of my great friends. I hope you enjoy his story.

Dennis Taylor, September 2011

CHAPTER ONE

THE END

The television was on, but the sound and pictures meant nothing to me. I couldn't tell you what was on or what it was about. I can't remember having any last thoughts in my head as I started to swallow the sleeping pills, washing them down with water. One after another, it all seemed very easy and very natural, as if I was preparing myself for a good night's sleep, except that I believed the number of pills I was swallowing would be enough to ensure it would be the last night's sleep I would ever have on this earth. If I had stopped to think about what I was doing, perhaps I would have panicked, but instead I just kept swallowing.

There was no great plan that Monday afternoon as I sat on the bed. I hadn't decided that this would be the day I would take my own life. In my depressed state, the thought had certainly floated around at the back of my mind. I saw it as my big get-out, a way of shedding all responsibilities for my actions with no comebacks. I'd had enough. It wasn't the act of a brave man, it was the act of a coward, but I didn't care. I felt trapped by the financial problems I had, the mounting debts which I just couldn't seem to conquer. I had borrowed money from all sorts of people in order to keep my head above water and stave off the inevitable, but the reality was that I was sinking fast. In fact, I felt like I was drowning.

Although the decision to start shovelling pills down my throat was a spur-of-the-moment thing, I had thought about taking my own life often enough in the weeks, months and years before the day actually arrived. I was very matter of fact about it, but I had no real idea of when it would happen, or of how I would go about the act of committing suicide. For some time I had felt a tremendous sense of despair at the predicament I found myself in. I also felt terribly guilty because I knew I had brought it all on myself; it was my actions and behaviour which had landed me in such a mess. I can see that now and I have no problem admitting it, but back then it was something I didn't really want to own up to. Instead, I was prepared to take the coward's way out, thinking only of myself and not of the hurt and despair I was about to cause to those closest to me.

At the time I felt that the crushing weight of the consequences of my actions was just too much for me to cope with. I had managed to carry on for some time, borrowing from Peter to pay off Paul, but on that day in March 2002, a few days after my 48th birthday, I'd had enough. The fight had gone out of me; I couldn't see a way out. I had finally been beaten by an addiction which had taken root many years before, when I was just a young man. An addiction that had begun before I became a professional snooker player and which stayed with me throughout my years as a high-earning sportsman. During that time, snooker became one of the most popular and lucrative sports in the country, watched by an audience of millions whenever it was televised in Britain and its popularity was growing fast around the world. Snooker had been my profession, but gambling had been my downfall. It had led to financial ruin and ultimately the misery which had finally driven me to try to take my own life.

Thinking about such a terrible act was one thing, but going through with it was quite something else. I can't speak for anyone else who has attempted suicide and tell you how they felt. I'm sure there are all sorts of reasons that push a human being towards such extreme action and they can be very different, but the one common emotion which I am sure exists is that of an overwhelming feeling of hopelessness. The feeling that no matter what you have tried in the past, or what has happened, there is nothing in the future that leads you to believe your problems can be solved, or that things will change and get better. To any sane, right-thinking person, this all might sound absolutely ridiculous. In writing about this whole episode now, all I am trying to do is lay out the facts, and to take responsibility for what I attempted to do to myself and what I ended up doing to others.

I have never wanted anyone to feel sympathy for what I did, and certainly don't believe I deserve any, because I still feel it was a terrible act of cowardice and totally selfish. I had problems in my life, but then so do other people. The vast majority of them do not choose to try taking their own lives. I was weak and self-obsessed when I made the decision. It was all about me when I'd squandered hundreds of thousands of pounds in an attempt to come out on top, to beat the bookies, beat the system, stay ahead of the game, whatever you like to call it. But, of course, the game I was involved in was for mugs. Mugs like me, and there was never a hope in hell that I was going to end up winning.

If you have an addiction, logic flies out of the window, and gambling had been my addiction for many years. When I was earning big money and at the height of my powers as a professional snooker player it had been easier to keep feeding the beast that had finally got the better of me. But in more recent times, with less money coming in, things had started to change dramatically. I knew it was happening, but I had been too weak to do anything about it. I had become a slave to my addiction, and like so many other gamblers I always believed that I could somehow get back, get myself straight. I kidded myself that I would have the big win which would solve all of my problems, except that in my case I probably needed several big wins to even stand a chance of climbing out of the hole I had dug for myself.

I didn't like myself, didn't like what I had become. I was deceitful and cunning. It was all about me and the madness I had created. I had no self-control, no discipline, no real thought for others or what the consequences of my actions would be for them. I had lied to those closest to me, including my own mother, and let them all down. Perhaps in some perverse way I thought that taking my own life would not only free me from my troubles, but also take away the burden from my family and friends. I wouldn't be around to cause any more problems; they could all get on with their lives without me and it would probably be better for them.

Looking back now, I think the real reason for making the decision that day was purely a selfish one, just as my gambling and the effect of what I was doing was selfish. I wasn't thinking of anyone else except me when I eventually started the process which I believed would lead to my death.

I was in a very strange place mentally, and my life seemed such a mess as I sat in my bedroom at home that afternoon, watching television but taking nothing in. There were pills on the bedside table, sleeping pills I had been prescribed. I'd had trouble sleeping for some time, and despite having taken the pills I still hadn't managed a good night's rest for months. I would often get up in the early hours of the morning with a feeling of hopelessness and depression hanging over me. The pills were supposed to help me rest my body and my mind, to rid me of whatever had been stopping me from relaxing properly. But I think the pills had too much to compete with, because my mind used to buzz with all sorts of thoughts in the middle of the night. That was when the gambling and money worries had a chance to haunt my thoughts without any real competition. They flooded my head, and the only way I could find to distract them was to wander downstairs, switch the television on, and stare blankly at the screen as I continuously flicked from channel to channel.

I don't know how many pills I actually swallowed, and I can't tell you the moment I drifted off and lost consciousness. My last thoughts were nothing out of the ordinary. I was calm throughout the whole process; there was no great emotion and no feeling of what I was actually doing. I was going to sleep forever, and in my own warped mind I had finally achieved a way out. I had left my problems behind. I was free.

CHAPTER TWO

ROCK BOTTOM

My eyes opened several hours later and immediately started filling with tears. Even in my dazed and groggy state, I quickly realised I had not passed on, leaving the world and my worries behind. I was still alive. The suicide bid had failed. I was in a hospital bed surrounded by some of my closest family and friends. The very people I had effectively tried to turn my back on forever.

I'd tried to kill myself, to end it all, but without once thinking of the hurt and pain I would cause in the process. My only attempt at trying to explain my actions had been to write a final scribbled note to my partner Jill as I attempted to put an end to my life in the house we shared together. I had stuck the message in an envelope and stuffed it with about £1,000 in cash. It was all the money I could lay my hands on at the time and I wanted her to have it. Willie Thorne, former snooker star, had hit rock bottom in more ways than one, and the cash had finally run out. After all the years of high earning and gambling, the only real money

I could give to the woman I loved was £1,000. It was pathetic in so many ways, and it was a measure of just how badly wrong things had gone for me. I can't remember exactly what I wrote, but I do know I told Jill how much I loved her and that after what I had done she would have to look after my mother and try to explain things to my kids. It was a terrible thing to do. I was taking the easy way out and leaving her to mop up the mess I had created. Quite apart from the fact that I was going to kill myself, I was asking Jill to take care of things for me when I'd gone. When I look back now, I can't believe what I did, but at the time I clearly wasn't thinking clearly at all. I was a desperate man.

Jill had been out of the house at the time I began swallowing pills, and her young son James, who was only just 11 years old at the time, had come home and found me sprawled on the bed. He assumed I was having an afternoon nap. Apparently, I was lying there with my mouth open making very strange noises. The television was blaring in the background and James clearly wasn't sure what to make of the situation. He'd seen me go up to the bedroom during the daytime before to have a nap, but clearly something about the way I looked and sounded prompted him into making a phone call to his mother. If James hadn't made that call it's quite likely I would never have opened my eyes again.

At the time Jill was at university as a mature student studying for a degree in human communication, and once James phoned her she headed home as quickly as she could. Ironically, that same day she had been trying to get hold of our doctor because she feared that, with all the different pills I had around at the time, mixing them up might have an adverse effect. Jill has since told me that as she made her way home, the thought that stayed with her during the journey was that in some way or other pills were the reason for me being crashed out on the bed in the way James had described to her.

As she arrived at the house James told her I was still in the bedroom upstairs, and as soon as Jill saw me alarm bells rang. Her 14-year-old daughter, Natalie, was also at the house by this time and Jill told her to get on the phone and call for an ambulance. It must have been horrendous for her to come home and find me unconscious on the bed. The envelope was still next to me with the note and cash poking out, and by this time it was clear to her that I had tried to take my own life. As she read the scrawled ramblings I had written down in an attempt to explain my actions, Jill still had the presence of mind to make sure that I got help as quickly as possible. She must have been beside herself with worry as she waited for the ambulance to arrive, talking to me in the hope that she would be able to bring me out of my stupor and that I would be able to cling on to my life.

The paramedics arrived and strapped me into a wheel-chair, which they managed to get down the stairs and then into the ambulance. Throughout all of this I was apparently opening and closing my eyes and Jill tried to talk to me, but I have no recollection of that. I was rushed to Leicester Royal Infirmary, with Jill in the ambulance still shocked by what had happened and what I'd tried to do. She didn't know whether I was going to live or die. She had come home to be confronted with a situation she should never have had to face, but I had not given a thought to those who mattered most to me, or what they would have to deal with because of what I had done.

When I did eventually open my eyes properly for the first time in the early hours of the morning I looked around the hospital bed I was lying in and realised I was not the only one crying. Jill was looking at me, smiling, but with tears in her eyes. My mum, Nancy, was there with my two brothers, Malcolm and Robert. So too was my good friend, John Hayes, who had been a huge help to me as I tried to get my finances sorted out. But I had concealed the true nature of my gambling debts, not only to him but to everyone around the bedside that day. All of them had tried to help and be supportive. All of them loved and cared for me, and yet they were the very people I had betrayed by attempting to take my own life.

The realisation of this provoked a whole new wave of remorse and made me feel absolutely awful. I had failed in life and now I had failed in my attempt to induce my own death. Worst still, I had let all these wonderful people down. The tears kept coming. I was so upset at what I had done and the hurt I must have caused; they, on the other hand, were just pleased to see me alive and the depth of love and kindness they all displayed was simply overwhelming. I kept saying sorry to all of them, the only word I could think of that went close to explaining just how I felt about what I had done. It was a very emotional scene, and to this day I carry the guilt of having been the person who caused so much pain and anguish to those who were closest to me.

There is no real excuse for what I did, none whatsoever. Of course, I was under financial pressure and there were problems which I felt at the time were closing in and about to overwhelm me. I was weak and chose to take a selfish way out, but I do not consider that to be an excuse for my actions. I was a coward, and for the rest of my life I will regret what I did and what I put others through.

In taking those pills I had not given a thought to the ripple effect such an action has on your loved ones. It was a quick solution to problems I had allowed to build up over a number of years. I was not a compulsive gambler, but I was certainly addicted to it, and addiction to anything is an illness. When it came to gambling, my logic had been pushed firmly to one side. It had started as a fun activity when I was a youngster and, during the boom years of snooker, the money I earned as a professional player allowed me to fund my addiction without ever really having to worry about the financial implications of what I was doing.

There always seemed to be a generous supply of cash coming in. But life as a top professional doesn't last forever. My hand-to-eye coordination deteriorated, the easier shots became harder, and victories were harder to come by. A new generation took over and I began to slip down the ladder. Consequently, the supply line of money I'd relied upon for so many years was suddenly no longer there.

It's never an easy thing for any sportsman to come to terms with; it's a struggle but sooner or later it comes to us all. My added problem was that I was gambling so heavily throughout my career. When it started to come to an end, I was no longer able to fund my addiction in the way I had throughout my playing days. As 'Willie Thorne the snooker player' it was always easy for me to get credit when I wanted to have a bet. I had a very decent earning capacity and people knew it. If I wanted to bet big, I could. It allowed me to gamble amounts that the ordinary man on the street couldn't. But anyone who loves to bet is the same, it's all relative to your income. Losing £100 on a horse can be just as disastrous to one individual as betting £1,000, £10,000 or £100,000 will be for others.

My gambling never stopped when my career as a snooker player ended; by that time it had too much of a hold on me. I never said to myself that I should take it easy, or pack the whole thing in. Instead, I just found new ways of making sure that I was able to have a bet, spending more money than I ever really had, and at the same time always kidding myself that I would be able to make it up and eventually get the sort of cash I needed. It's the classic gambler's delusion, where any logic and common sense is put firmly to one side while you go chasing winning bets. Of course, it never happens, and in my case I sank deeper and deeper into trouble, became more and more depressed, and eventually reached rock bottom.

I was in complete despair lying in that hospital bed as I began to take in exactly what I'd done. It was very difficult to come to terms with my actions. You hear all the time about people committing suicide and what drove them to it, but this wasn't someone else I was reading about in a newspaper. This was me, and somehow I had to start thinking about what I was going to do next.

Perhaps I was still in shock, or suffering the after-effects of my actions, but just four days after trying to take my own life I went ahead with a speaking engagement I'd been booked to appear at in Nottingham. Don't ask me why I did it. Perhaps it was a subconscious need to get back to normality as quickly as I could, and I saw that as a very normal part of my life at the time. I was due to speak alongside the former England rugby union international, Rory Underwood, and sure enough I turned up to do just what was expected of me. Jill came with me, as did my good friend, Bernard Prewitt. Obviously both of them knew what had gone on with me, but nobody else in the room that night did. As far as they were concerned it was just a case of Willie Thorne turning up to speak.

I have always loved mixing with the public and over the years they have been very good to me. I think I have a natural rapport with people and I have made a point of doing things like signing autographs and taking the time to stop and talk. I think it's really nice that they are interested in me, and I know that if it wasn't for them I would not have had a career. The support and kindness I have been given over the years is really appreciated.

Being a 'celebrity' has never been a problem for me. I suppose I've always been a bit of a performer, whether it's been with a snooker cue in my hand or, in more recent years, doing my after-dinner speaking and hosting events. However, I don't really know how I got through that particular engagement in Nottingham. I think I must have done it on auto-pilot, because I was really in no fit state. Don't get me wrong, nobody was pointing a gun to my head and saying, 'You have to turn up and go through with this'. It was my decision and I think I just wanted to prove to myself and others that I was ready to carry on. It was stupid really, because that simply wasn't the case. I felt dreadful in the car and very unsure of myself which, given the events of the previous few days, was not surprising. But as soon as I got to the venue and stepped out of the car I somehow managed to put on my public face and slipped into the role of guest speaker with the same sort of ease I'd always done. I went through the whole evening talking and smiling, signing autographs and generally doing exactly what the people who had turned up expected of me, but as soon as I got back into the car for the drive home it was a very different story.

I was all over the place, and the emotional turmoil I'd gone through started to take its toll. For the previous few hours I had been happy to adopt my public persona and probably felt protected by it. I had an audience and I could play the part of a well-known former sportsman. I'd slipped into my routine and performed it as if nothing had happened, but once I got back in the car there was no audience and the people who were riding with me knew exactly what I had done just days ago. I couldn't pretend in front of them, they saw me for what I was and I found that difficult. I felt so ashamed of what I had put Jill through, and yet there she was giving me the love and support I needed. All she wanted was for me to be happy, to recover from the trauma of trying to take my own life and for us to start to rebuild our lives together.

Despite my fragile state, I was still aware of having to take care of certain situations which arose as a consequence of my actions. News of my stay in hospital had leaked out, but the real reason for me going there had not been reported. I think that while I was in the hospital somebody might have seen me being wheeled along one of the corridors. Obviously, I was well known in the area and it didn't take long before news came out. I knew I had to do something pretty quickly to nip the whole thing in the bud, and so I made a call to a very well-known publicist who I knew and explained what I'd done and what had happened. He got straight onto the case and issued some sort of statement confirming I'd been in hospital, but saying that the cause of my brief stay there had been because of a mix-up with medication I was taking. The story appeared in the tabloids, but with an explanation that helped gloss over the whole thing and end any rumours that had been floating around suggesting I had tried to commit suicide.

The article appeared at the end of March with carefully worded quotes from me. 'I had been taking pain killers for irritable bowel syndrome,' I explained. 'They made me woozy but didn't kill the pain.

'I knew some time had passed since I took the last lot and so I took some more. The next thing I remember is waking up in hospital. I feel a complete bloody fool.

'I feel fine now. I have absolutely no reason to wish to take my own life.'

That seemed to put and end to the story, and it was a relief for me to have a professional take control of the situation and smooth the whole thing over.

I had been saved from killing myself, but I was still very much aware that my problems hadn't gone away. It was now up to me to start dealing with them. Strange as it might sound, I think that once I had come to terms with the fact that I was still alive and that I still had to cope with my financial problems, I also felt as though a weight had been lifted from my shoulders. I had tried for too long to hide my dirty financial washing, and I was now going to have to face up to things and somehow deal with the situation I was in, simply by virtue of the fact that I was still alive and my get-out plan hadn't worked.

But my debts weren't the only thing I had to confront during the days that followed my attempted suicide. I have always suffered from depression, and even to this day that is still the case. I don't think one particular thing triggered the depression, but it is a condition I have learned to cope with over the years. As I have mentioned, the fact that I decided to try and end it all was not a pre-meditated act, and although I'd thought about the possibility and even the way in which I would go about killing myself, the exact time and place that it should happen was never something I planned. The overwhelming feeling of hopelessness that surrounded me at the time was probably what prompted me into the action I took. I had debts, I was no longer 'Willie Thorne the snooker player', I wanted a way out and the way out I chose was a crazy one.

Coming to terms with all of that wasn't easy, and coming to terms with the tremendous guilt I felt was even harder. I realised how awful I'd been to Jill, my family and to my good friend John Hayes who had helped me so much and was working hard to sort out my problems. I'd put them through so much pain and anguish.

Jill's tremendous love was the thing that helped me most as I attempted to rebuild my life. I wanted to keep on saying sorry for what I'd done, and I know that I became very clingy after the incident. When I walked through the front door of our house I just wanted to retreat from the world and have nothing to do with it. I didn't want to take any responsibility for many day-to-day things that are a part of any couple's lives. For instance, I didn't want to open the post or answer the phone. I only really felt safe and comfortable when Jill was around me. Don't get me wrong, I was still able to go out of the house and put on my public face. That was never really a problem for me. It was when I went home and the door closed that I really had my biggest problems, because I still felt unsure of myself and what I was going to do about my life. I was very solemn, very apologetic and generally very low.

In many ways I assumed a double identity at the time. Nobody other than my family and close friends would have thought I had a care in the world. Being able to mask my real feelings like that was something I had always done to some degree. Even when I was playing in tournaments and had money troubles, nobody would have realised that was the case just by looking at my face or seeing the way I acted. To anyone on the outside I was just the same old Willie they'd always known, but sometimes I'd go back to my hotel room and my head would be in my hands.

While I have often suffered from depression, conversely, I have also always been a bit of a joker and perhaps I've overemphasised that at times during my life. Maybe the reality of it was that I used the jokiness as a front to mask exactly what was going on and how I was really feeling. I always found it a lot easier to live my life behind the public face of Willie Thorne. I could almost forget my worries when I did something like hosting a dinner, speaking to the public or taking part in a charity golf day. I would ease into celebrity mode; it was almost a performance.

That's not to say I didn't like the public, because I did, but I suppose I also liked what they gave me, which was a sense of worth. I knew that my life was a mess, that I owed thousands of pounds and that I had screwed things up, but they didn't. To them I was just 'good old Willie Thorne,' someone who liked to have a laugh and a joke and was always bright and breezy. It was common knowledge that I'd had money problems in the past, but by the time I attempted to take my life, most people thought that was all behind me and as far as they were concerned I was moving into a new era in my life. I had never been just a one-dimensional sportsman; I had enough going for me to make sure there was life after snooker and a pretty decent life at that. So in many ways I played up to that image and when I was out of the house and 'performing', I could lose myself in the moment and forget things to some extent, but when I came home and walked through the front door, reality enveloped me.

I was very secretive about the extent of my problems, keeping the truth from everyone. I admitted and owned up to some of what was going on, but not all of it. Not the fact that I had money lenders on my back needing to have their payments met. Not the fact that I was borrowing from all sorts of people to pay-off others, and not the fact that

I was seriously contemplating suicide. By the time I swallowed those pills on that March afternoon I was in a very dark place mentally; I was in shreds, and once I had come out of hospital my mind was still in a very fragile state.

Without the love and support of Jill I'm not sure what I would have done. She's very intelligent and has got the heart of a lion. She was so incredibly understanding and when I needed someone to lean on, she was there for me. Jill stayed positive throughout, and gave me all the support she could. I sometimes wonder if another woman would have walked away from it all – she certainly had every right to and I couldn't have blamed her if she had. Jill had also put up with a lot from me before I tried to top myself. There were times when the burden of having so many money worries just seemed to weigh me down and I wasn't a particularly nice person to live with. I was very grumpy around the house, but she coped with my moods and then when I came out of hospital she was there for me, giving me all the love I needed. Unconditional love. Jill just wanted to care and look after me, something I will never forget and for which I will always be grateful.

Perhaps the biggest single thing that helped me so much during my recovery period was deciding that we would get married. We had been together since 1994 and deciding to tie the knot in January 2003 felt like absolutely the right thing to do. It was a marvellous feeling to be with someone who I loved so much and who cared and understood me even after all I had put her through. I had lied to Jill and to John Hayes about the extent of my problems. Who would have blamed the pair of them for turning their backs on me after what I'd done? Happily for me, neither of them did, and both would go on to play a big part in helping me to rebuild my life both emotionally and, in John's case, financially. I had a lot to apologise for and there were many crying sessions after my attempted suicide, not least with my three children from my first marriage to their mother, Fiona. I have twin boys, Tristan and Kieran, as well as a daughter, Tahli. All three had already had to experience me leaving home when my marriage to Fiona ended, and I'd then put them through the trauma of having their father trying to take his own life.

"Dad, why did you want to leave us?" Kieran asked me one day and, quite simply, I didn't have an answer. We were both in tears as he tried to come to terms with what I had done and I tried to explain what had driven me to such an action, but the truth was that I wasn't able to fully understand it myself. This was my son, how on earth could I have thought of doing what I did? There was simply no excuse for it, and there still isn't. In trying to take my own life I didn't set out to emotionally scar the people I loved most, but that's exactly what I would have done had James, Jill and Natalie not taken the action they did.

It was still very hard for all of them to come to terms with what had happened and a lot was left unsaid. There were no family group sessions where we talked openly about my actions. We simply all tried to get on with our lives again and act as normally as we could. Throughout all of this time, they were the strong ones. It couldn't have been easy for them, but their love and care for me made a tremendous difference. I was often full of self-doubt when

I was at home. I needed Jill beside me and I needed her strength. I clung to her for emotional support and she gave it. I wanted to be around her and if she wasn't in the house I sometimes felt uncomfortable. I realise now that it was all part of the fall-out from what had happened, but at the time it must have been difficult for Jill to have to cope with.

One other person who was special during this period and who has been throughout my entire life was my mum. She has always been there for me, giving me love and support. She didn't deserve to be put through the experience of her son trying to take his own life, but her only thoughts when I had survived the attempt were to care for me and give me the sort of stability she always had done. In stark contrast to me, she had never owed a penny in her life and had done a wonderful job of bringing up her three children, so why did she end up with a son like me who, for so many years, just never understood the value of money despite being lucky enough to make an awful lot of it?

The truth is I don't have an answer, and I suspect I never will. I still sometimes sit and wonder why I did some of the things I did. Why I succumbed to my gambling addiction and why I let more than £1.5 million slip through my fingers because of it. I've had lots of ups and many downs during my life, huge highs and disastrous lows. I have done a lot of things that I am not proud of and which I will regret until the day I die. Despite having the good fortune to be a naturally gifted snooker player who had a wonderful career in the game, I never achieved what I should have as a professional. I feel that at various stages in my life I have failed as a father, as a husband and as a son. My weaknesses have cost me both emotionally and financially, but I also realise that in recent years, with the help of my family and friends, I have been able to put right some of the wrongs and to learn to look to the future instead of wallowing in the past. However, the past, both good and bad, is what has brought me to this point and, rather than choosing to ignore it, I have decided to explore it.

CHAPTER THREE

TAKING MY CUE

Like most other boys with an older brother there was always an element of competition between Malcolm and I. He was almost four years my senior and then there was a gap of around 10 years between me and my younger brother Robert. I used to look up to Malcolm, and we were always playing different games together. Football, cricket, running, jumping. . . you name it we did it. He wasn't just a brother, he was also a good mate. He was pretty sporty and there was no doubt that, if he had put his mind to it, Malcolm could probably have become a professional cricketer – he was that good. Although we played all sorts of things and got stuck into pursuits like fishing, which he was also very good at, there were never any real arguments between us and we never fell out. I wanted to beat him when it was a one-on-one game, and I liked to prove I was able to compete with him, but it never spilled over and I think there was always a very healthy regard for each other's ability.

I certainly admired Malcolm, and I looked up to him as

a youngster. He always seemed so much more mature and grown up, just as you would expect an older brother to be. He was a naturally gifted sportsman – whether he had to use a bat or a ball, it didn't really matter, he seemed to take to anything. Anything, that is, except snooker. For some reason or other he never really got into the game and showed no great interest in it. That was certainly not the case with me. I'm not quite sure why, but when I first set eyes on a snooker table I immediately wanted to start potting balls, and the wonderful thing was that I was able to do just that. I was a natural.

It all started at the age of about nine or ten – I honestly can't remember exactly when it was, only that one Christmas my parents bought a mini snooker table for Malcolm, which we both used to play on. It measured six foot by three and as soon as it arrived I was mesmerised by it. I started potting five and six balls at a time and pretty quickly became hooked on the game. Malcolm, on the other hand, was far less enthusiastic and, although he could pot a couple of balls without any problems, he never seemed to be able to build on it and, as a consequence of that, I think, the game never really captured his imagination. The opposite was true for me and the other great thing was that I had managed to find something that I was actually better at than Malcolm. I had no real trouble beating him, and although the games were always very friendly, there's no doubt that winning feels even sweeter when it's against your older brother. It was also probably a huge boost to my ego and confidence at that early stage in my life.

Of course, potting balls on a small table is very different

to doing it on the real thing. The scale and dimension of a full-size snooker table is very different, not to mention the size of the cue you're using and the weight of the balls you have to try and hit. In the summer following the Christmas in which the mini table arrived, we went on a family holiday with some friends to the York House Hotel in Eastbourne on the south coast. Each night after our evening meal the two families would go down to a room on the ground floor of the hotel which housed a snooker table. My dad Joseph, who was always known as Bill, would have a quick frame or two with his friend and then we would all go off for a walk. As soon as I set eyes on the table I wanted to have a go at potting the balls. It was so much bigger than the table I'd been used to playing on with Malcolm, but I still felt confident of being able to replicate the sort of scoring action I had managed on our little table at home. From the first day we were there I began to ask if I could have a go. The table seemed huge but, far from being intimidated, all I wanted to do was pot some balls. I wasn't scared at the thought of having a go, just excited.

The allure of this immovable object, lights illuminating the green baize and lending a mysterious air amid the darkness, was instant. I couldn't wait to play on it, but that pleasure kept being denied me. I must have nagged my mother so much that she actually went and asked the man who owned the place if it would be alright for me to play some shots on the table, but when he looked at me and saw how old I was the warning lights must have started flashing in his mind. Not unreasonably, he politely told my mum that he didn't think it would be possible because I might rip the cloth. You could understand why he refused because, although I was quite tall for my age, I was still only a kid, and he had no idea whether I could hold a cue properly, let alone pot a ball. It was agonising for me, because I had complete confidence in my own ability, even at that age, and I knew there was no way I'd have ripped the cloth with my cue. All I wanted to do was experience the thrill of playing on a proper table for the first time in my life.

My pleadings went on every night, and every night my mother would repeat what the owner had said and then tell me that I wasn't allowed to play on the table. We'd gone there for a two-week holiday, and on the evening before we were due to return home my dad's mate somehow managed to persuade the owner that he should let me have a go. I suppose he was thinking that if anything did go wrong, we were all going home the next day, so it wasn't going to be a case of having it hanging over us for the rest of the holiday. The owner relented, and I was allowed to take one of the cues and start potting the balls just as I had done at home on the mini table. Everything was bigger but the basics remained the same, and I found that even on a big table I was hitting shots all over the place and they were coming off. It was a real thrill and the game really captured my imagination. I have never forgotten the sheer joy of potting balls that evening.

Years later, in 1985, when I was competing in the Mercantile Credit Classic tournament, watched by an audience of millions on television, my mother took it upon herself to make a phone call to that same hotel in Eastbourne. She was watching the match on TV and began to think back to that day in the 1960s when I'd potted those balls and played for the first time on a full-size table. She decided she would phone the hotel and let them know that her son, Willie Thorne, had first experienced the thrill of playing on a proper table when I stayed in Eastbourne all those years before. She actually spoke to the son of the guy who had refused to let me play back then, and mum told me that when she got through she could hear commentary on my match in the background as they watched the same television pictures she had on in her house. Once they realised that she was genuine and it wasn't some sort of prank call, they got very excited about the fact that I had taken my first real steps in snooker playing on their table. So much so that they asked me to make a personal appearance down there some time later, which I duly did. I actually won the Mercantile that year, and when I went down to the south coast they gave me a great welcome, with lots of the locals turning out to say hello. It was lovely to revisit the place, and typical of my mother to think of doing something like that.

Mum has always played a big part in my life, and certainly her love and support have been so important to me over the years. I'd be lying if I said my parents had an idyllic marriage. All couples have their ups and downs, and my mum and dad had their fair share. I can still remember some of the rows I would hear around the house from a very early age. I look back now and realise that things did not always go well in their relationship, but I suppose that at the time I just pushed the whole thing to one side and got on with my life. The raised voices were just a part of my upbringing, but I didn't grow up in a horrible atmosphere, and my parents loved and looked after all of their children. The truth is that mum and dad had their problems and sometimes they spilled over. He could become quite physical after a few drinks and none of us were spared this violent side of his character. It wasn't nice hearing them row, and perhaps I understand why it happened more now than I did then.

Despite all of this, my mother and father always did the best they could for us boys and as a result I think I had a pretty good childhood overall. I was certainly given a degree of freedom and support throughout my time as a kid and then into my teenage years that I suspect a lot of other kids wouldn't have had. We weren't well off, but there was always food on the table and we were always comfortable.

I was born on 4th March 1954 and grew up in a village called Anstey on the outskirts of Leicester. We had a very nice, comfortable three-bedroom home and Dad worked as a miner at Desford colliery. He was a big, gruff, rough-and-ready sort of man who could be very kind at times, but who was also aggressive, stubborn and always wanted things done his way. This part of my father's character seemed to take on an even darker side when he'd had a few drinks, and he was not averse to raising his hands to us all, including my mother. I loved him and respected him, but quite often he just didn't seem to have a clue about social niceties or the way he should treat his own family. He had worked down the mines and his language could be fruity to say the least. The trouble was that Dad never really knew when it was inappropriate to let go with a few choice words, and he often did this in completely the wrong environment. I lost count of the times I felt embarrassed by his behaviour.

I owe a lot to him, though, because, like my mum, he was very supportive when it came to my snooker in the early days and then later when I turned professional. He was a grafter and made sacrifices for me and all the family. In many ways it was because of the route his working life took that I was able to get involved in snooker to the degree that I did. He spent time with me when I was a kid and we would often go off on shooting trips together in the Leicestershire countryside, but throughout his life he was never really able to understand the game of snooker. Like any parent, he wanted his son to win, but when it came to the tactics of a match and understanding the subtleties of the game, he really didn't have a clue. Whenever he played he would just try to make sure he potted the ball and didn't worry about the next shot. That didn't stop him telling me what I should do, though! But I think he was very proud of me and certainly enjoyed sharing the pleasure in my successes I had as an amateur and then a professional player.

Towards the end of his life, when he'd been left in a pretty bad way after suffering several strokes, he became very mellow and was a shadow of the man I'd known as a kid growing up and then into my early adult life. The fight had gone out of him and I suspect that there were moments he reflected on his life and the way his actions might have affected those closest to him. I have no doubt at all that my father loved his children. I also have no doubt that the way he sometimes acted towards us and to my mother became true regrets in his later life. He'd certainly treated my mother badly on occasions, and some of the things he did to her were unbelievable.

When I was a young man making my way in the game of snooker my parents' marriage was pretty much over, but the two of them still ran a pub together. I was away one night and the two of them had apparently had another row. My dad had been drinking, and I later learned that he had locked my mother in the cellar for about four or five hours. Mum certainly had to put up with a lot from him – indeed, at that time he'd moved another woman into the pub to live with him.

Despite the treatment my mother suffered at his hands throughout their time together she still found it within her heart to take my dad in many years later and look after him when he'd had his strokes. She even had a special ramp built to help get his wheelchair in and out of the house and, although their relationship as man and wife had long since ended, she would cook his meals, look after him and generally make his existence so much more comfortable than it would otherwise have been during the twilight of his life. It may sound strange to some people that she would do something like that after the way he'd treated her, but it was typical of my mother. She has always been the sort of person who will help you, something she has certainly done for me on countless occasions over the years, even though I must have caused her so much pain, anguish and worry with a lot of the things I've got up to.

I went to Anstey Martin Primary school, and it was in the juniors that I really began to develop a love of sport, helped by a couple of the teachers there who encouraged me to pursue my interest in football and cricket. I was pretty good academically and eventually did enough to get myself a decent job, but it was always sport which captured my imagination, and I tended to plunge myself into anything going, so long as it involved being active and competitive. With Malcolm always on hand to play sport and games with me, I had a great time. Malcolm was not as outgoing as me and very soon I realised that I liked being a bit of a show-off. Not in a nasty way, I was just simply someone who didn't mind having an audience and who felt comfortable talking to people.

I was a pretty good centre-forward and a good enough cricketer to be involved at county level, playing for Leicestershire colts. I also used to like playing basketball. The two sports teachers at the school, George Kershaw and Dave Geary, put a lot of time and effort into making sure us kids enjoyed our sport, and in my case I suppose they were the ones who lit the blue touch paper. There's no doubt that they developed my interest in all things sporting, and I'm sure that a lot of my confidence sprang from the fact that I was a naturally good sportsman. I could express myself though playing games and achieving things on the playing field. There was a sense of excitement and achievement involved and I found the mixture very attractive, especially as I didn't really have any problems being pretty good at most of the sports I tried. It all came easily and it made sport all the more enjoyable for me; that and the fact that I became used to winning, which I loved. I liked being able to do things well and got a buzz from getting good results from the games I played.

I was also a pretty good runner, and at one point I was probably the best in the school. There is an incident that I can vividly remember to this day and I mention it because I think that, even at such an early age, it illustrated something about my personality and my fear of failure.

I was due to run a race and was pretty confident that I was going to be the winner, but I got off to a bad start and knew instantly that I was not going to make up the lost ground in time to win. Instead of just carrying on and trying to do the best I could, I pretended I was injured and pulled out. I simply couldn't face the thought of failure and when I look back on my career as a snooker player, perhaps that same fear was often at the back of my mind when it came to tournaments. I would often 'twitch' (mess up shots I would normally expect to get) at vital stages of an important match and I didn't have the mental strength I should have had to go with my natural talent.

That talent soon began to emerge. Having got the snooker bug with my parents' purchase of that mini table and then my brief experience of the real thing in Eastbourne, it soon became clear that this was a game which I not only enjoyed playing, but which I was also very good at. Both of my parents could see this as well, and for my 14th birthday mum went out and bought something that is still a treasured possession to this day. It was a maple wood Walter Lindrum snooker cue, and it was to stay with me, with a few tweaks along the way, throughout my professional snooker career. In fact, in the years which followed the cue virtually became an extension of my arm when I was playing in tournaments around the world. It was my most precious and treasured possession. It would go everywhere with me. If I was playing an event, I wouldn't let it out of my sight, and if a fire alarm went off in a hotel I was staying at, the cue was always the first thing I grabbed as I left the room. I always looked after it and would never let anyone else have a shot with it. I was so protective of the cue, and treated the thing as though it was a baby. It may sound silly and totally over the top to some people, but, believe me, when you start to play the game seriously having the right cue is so important. You have to feel comfortable and confident when you go to the table, and anything that disrupts that comfort and puts you out of your routine can have a really bad effect on the way you play.

I did have one horrible moment during the years that I used it when I returned to my house very late one night after an event and, feeling exhausted, sloped off to bed. The next morning I woke up in panic realising that I couldn't remember bringing my cue into the house with me when I'd got back the night before. I raced downstairs and ran out to the car before seeing my cue, still safely in its case, propped up against the side of my car. I cannot describe the sense of relief I felt when I saw it. If the cue had been lost or stolen it would have been a terrible blow, and without doubt it would have had an awful effect on my game as I tried to get used to a new one. Most players would need at least a week playing regularly to get used to a new cue and some are never quite the same after switching from their old faithful because you get so used to your own and it becomes part of what you are when you go to the table. If I'd lost the cue at the height of my career and had to use a new one, I wouldn't have been able to make a 50 break with it. Thankfully, it stayed with me throughout my career, but I had no idea as a 14-year-old kid that it was going to play such an important part in my life.

My mum had gone to the local sports shop in Leicester in order to make the purchase and had agreed to pay for it in instalments. It cost three pounds, two shillings and six pence in old money (about £30 in today's money), and it turned out to be one of the most important things she ever bought. At the time I was just delighted to have a proper snooker cue to play with, but there was no point in having it unless I could put the thing to good use. Without my mum and dad knowing I would sometimes take the bus into Loughborough to go to 'The Shack,' a billiard hall that used to be situated above Burton's the tailors, and using some of my pocket money I would go and play on the tables there and practise some shots. I loved the experience of it all, and mixing with the men who played there regularly only helped my game improve. Of course, I sometimes came out of the place completely penniless, because I'd lost all my money playing challenge matches against some of the regulars. That was all part of growing up and it didn't really bother me, even if it did mean having to walk home because I didn't have enough money for the bus fare.

At about the same time, fate played a part in helping me to really improve my game. The colliery at Desford was closed down and my dad was made redundant. He didn't really know what he was going to do and was out of work for a while until the chance to become the steward at the Anstey Conservative Club presented itself. The chairman of the club happened to work with my mother and he was also a friend. In the end I think he used his influence to get the chance for my father, who gratefully took it, even though I think he only ever saw it as a bit of a stop-gap job while he looked for something else. The wonderful thing from my point of view was the fact that the club had a full-size snooker table, and it immediately gave me the opportunity to improve my game. I used to help dad with racking up and stocking the shelves and then I used to have about an hour and a half to myself to practise before he opened up in the afternoon, and then when he locked up after that I would stay at the club and play some more snooker, before he came back in the evening to open up again.

In those days if you wanted to play snooker on proper tables you could only really do it in three places: the conservative club, the working men's club and the billiard hall. There may have been the odd table knocking around in a pub, but in terms of more organised matches and decent players it was really only the three types of clubs that provided the kind of setup for you to play competitive matches and learn about the game. The best players tended to congregate in billiard halls, places that were usually also populated by vagabonds and thieves. The next best players were in the working men's clubs and the third tier of players frequented conservative clubs.

Nevertheless, having the opportunity to play on the table at Anstey was perfect for me, and one of the members there was a very good player indeed. His name was Joe Young and he came from Newcastle. He was able to make 50 breaks, which was impressive by conservative club standards. He took the time and trouble to encourage me and also to offer advice. He knew how to screw the ball back and play with side, so I learnt simply by watching him and copying what he was doing. He also told me one day that it was no good just potting the red to get on a colour. You have to get on a colour on the right side so that you get to the next red. It may sound simple enough but you'd be surprised how many people just don't think that far ahead and are just obsessed with trying to pot a ball. My dad was a prime example of this, and because of that there was never a hope of him really being able to build breaks. So from a pretty early stage in my development as a snooker player I was taught to think two shots ahead of what I was about to do on the table. My cue-ball control was always good, and I understood instinctively that it was important for me to have to take charge of the white as I went about trying to build decent breaks.

I used to love playing on the table at the club, and my game improved as a result of all the practice I was able to get. It soon became clear I was a good player, and the other members of the club used to watch me play matches there if they weren't actually playing against me, but my enthusiasm for the game began to cause a bit of a problem. I was on the table so much that I started to put a few noses out of joint, because the members weren't able to play as frequently as they wanted to. I would finish one game and then go to the board that hung on the wall next to the table to chalk my name up again, so that when the table became available I was on it again. In the end I was banned from playing, or at least, they stopped me from using the table at certain times. It ended with me being allowed to play for an hour from 11am at weekends and in school holidays, and then in the evenings throughout the week I was given another hour to play, between 5pm and 6pm. These two-hour periods were the times when it was quiet at the club, but it didn't really matter to me because I knew that even with the restrictions they'd imposed I was still able to get in half a dozen frames each day, and my game continued to improve rapidly.

Running the club gave my dad the chance to learn new skills. He discovered what was needed to look after such a place and it wasn't hugely different to being in control of a pub, so that was a natural next step. It wasn't an easy tenancy for him because he took control of a huge pub in the middle of a council estate in Braunston called The Shoulder of Mutton and later its name was changed to The Falcon. It was a massive place with lots of rooms above the bar and it also had the reputation of being a bit of a rough house where there could sometimes be trouble. It didn't seem to daunt my dad, and to his credit he very quickly sorted that side of it out, letting some of the punters know in no uncertain terms that they were not welcome. So he turned a pub that was pretty awful into a good one. Because there were so many big rooms in the place it didn't take too long before one of them was accommodating a snooker table, and I was able to continue my playing education with hours of uninterrupted practice.

I was still young but had left school at the age of 15 and was working as an estimator for a local glass company called Norman & Underwood. I really enjoyed myself there;

the work offered a degree of freedom and I wasn't confined to an office and a desk which suited me. I was out and about meeting people and dealing with different situations; I was given responsibility and I liked that. I think I was pretty good at the job, and something else that I knew I was pretty good at was snooker. My game had come on in leaps and bounds and I wasn't just playing at a local level any more. After leaving school I had won the national under-16 championships and it was clear I had natural flair for the game.

It wasn't just having a snooker table to hand at the pub that helped my improvement. The biggest reason for my continued progress was that, even as a schoolkid, I had made the move into a much higher standard of snooker, when I became a regular at a billiard hall in Leicester called Osborne's. As I have mentioned, the highest standard of snooker was played in billiard halls at this time, but I was only 15 and these places also had a bit of a reputation for attracting disreputable characters. The place would be busy throughout the week and weekends. It was situated near the market in Leicester and you would get quite a few of the traders going in there, but it also had its fair share of people who made their money by various other means, not all of them legal. There was also a very definite gambling culture at the club, with bets being placed on games that were being played. I used to go in there on Saturdays at first while I was still at school.

By this time, my mother knew just how keen I was on the game and she also realised that, having bought me my cue, I needed to find somewhere to use it playing against other good players. She knew all about Osborne's and, being my mother, she also felt the need to try and make sure that I was looked after. I'm sure she realised that it was inevitable that I would gravitate towards a billiard hall, and so she rang Mrs Osborne to say that I was a keen snooker player and wanted the opportunity to play regularly. I don't know exactly what she said, but it was clear to 'Mrs O', as I would always call her, that my mother was asking whether she would keep an eye out for me and generally make sure I came to no harm. I think she also wanted to make sure I steered clear of some of the more unsavoury characters she thought might be in there. I think Mrs Osborne was quite amazed by the fact that a mother should take the time and trouble to call her, and she apparently assured my mum that I would be fine. So I began to play my snooker at the club and mix with players who were of a much higher standard than any I had encountered before.

Within a year of going there on a regular basis I was by far and away the best player at Osborne's, taking over from Brian Cakebread, the guy who had previously held that mantle, and who was an excellent player. Brian was very good to me. He became my coach in those early days and there's no doubt I owe a lot to him. Like me, he loved snooker, but Brian also had another passion, one that I would also start to associate with during my time at Osborne's. He loved to have a bet.

CHAPTER FOUR

BITTEN BY THE BUG

To say that Brian Cakebread liked a bit of a bet is an understatement. He was a compulsive gambler and would bet any time of day, seven days a week. He was a lovely guy, and I can't in any way blame him for my own gambling addiction, but the fact is that someone like Brian fitted perfectly into a place like Osborne's, because of the betting culture. Going there when I did dramatically improved my snooker and it allowed me to play against much better players, but it was also where the gambling bug really began to bite.

Don't get me wrong, I have nothing but affection for the place. Ernie Osborne and Mrs O were a lovely couple who kept the place as neat and tidy as they could, and the 22 snooker tables were always in very good condition. About five of those tables were always in use for gambling, where side wagers on matches were made, and it wasn't too long before I became involved in them. It was a great way of making extra money and I had enough confidence in my own ability to know that it wouldn't take me long to get up there with the best players the club had to offer, including the best of them all – Brian. I think he immediately saw something in me as a player that told him I was going to be pretty good as well. He passed on some good tips to me during my time at the club and when he became my coach I rapidly began to make progress.

Brian was a compulsive gambler. He'd get up in the morning and would be betting on the dogs between 11am and 1pm, then he would be in the bookies during the afternoon until about 6pm before switching to the dogs again. After that little lot he might move on to a casino and continue gambling there. In between all of this he would find time to practise with me, and that was pretty much what his day consisted of. With a betting shop right next to the billiard hall it didn't take much effort to stroll there and gamble on the horses in the afternoon, and I soon got into the habit myself. I don't believe that going to Osborne's made me into a gambler. I suspect that as with all addictions there is something within the individual that is predisposed to wanting to carry on that way. All I know is that from a pretty young age I got a buzz out of gambling, and betting on horse races gave me the biggest buzz of all.

The club was full of the sort of characters you would have expected to find in any billiard hall up and down the country at that time in Britain. We're talking about the late 1960s and early 1970s and, apart from finding a high standard of snooker being played in Osborne's, it was also the kind of place where you could get all sorts of things.

If you wanted a cheap television or radio, someone in there would be able to provide it. Clothes, furniture, cars, bikes. . . you name it and someone would quite literally come up with the goods.

So many of the people there seemed to have nicknames, and quite a few of them became good friends who would later follow me to tournaments around the country when I became a professional. People like 'The Red-Faced Man from Braunston', 'Billy the Dip', 'Captain John', 'Stuttering Vic', 'Traffic Lights', 'Relentless Reg' and 'Handbags Gary'. They all added to the general atmosphere of the place and I enjoyed being around them and being part of what was going on.

I was young and perhaps a bit impressionable, but at the same time I not only liked the atmosphere of the place I also got on really well with the people there. I very quickly became accepted and enjoyed their company. Although we all used to play snooker, a conversation about betting was never very far away; whether it concerned having a wager on the games that were taking place at the club, or talking about the form of various horses, gambling gossip was always part of the scene at Osborne's.

I knew some of the people who went to the club were not exactly your conventional sort of guys. They certainly weren't a bunch of nine-to-five office workers who nipped in for a quick game of snooker. Many of them earned their money in slightly unconventional ways, some of which were not legal, but it was all part and parcel of the scene. It was the sort of place where people were always having a laugh and a joke and you were accepted for what you were. I might have mixed with some rogues, but my main reason for going to the club in the first place was to play snooker. I knew I had ability and could beat people who had been playing the game for a lot longer than me, but I also wanted to learn more and improve my own game, which I started to do. But along with my snooker education came another kind of knowledge, as I became more and more immersed in the horse-racing scene.

There was a guy called Greg Baxter who played at Osborne's, and the thing that really impressed me about him wasn't his snooker playing, it was his approach to gambling. Greg wasn't the sort of punter who would just place a bet and hope that the horse won, he had to know all about the horse before he backed it. He was the first person I'd come across who studied form and he was pretty successful at it. In many ways he was probably the reason I got more and more involved in racing and, of course, there were plenty of other people in the club who already shared my developing interest in horses. I might have been under starter's orders, but they were way down the track, regular punters.

In order to bet you needed money. There were no easy lines of credit available to people in those days, but although I was still young I always had cash on me. I had my job, but I was also making money from the matches I played and that side of my income began to steadily grow, along with my prowess on the snooker table. My game was getting better by the day and I was beginning to earn a reputation as one of the best young players in the country.

It was all very different in those days and you have to

remember that, although snooker was a popular sport with lots of people, it certainly didn't have the profile it would later gain during the boom years of the 1980s. It was still very much confined to the club scene, with local leagues providing much of the competitive element of the game. It wasn't really seen on television and hardly got a mention in the newspapers or on radio back then. The people who played the game kept up to date with what was going on by reading the trade snooker and billiard magazines, and it was through these that my name was slowly becoming better known.

Having won the under-16 national championship I went on to win three under-19 championships in a row. I also won the Leicestershire championship when I was 17 years old, but because I wasn't yet 18 they stripped me of the title! Because of that I decided that I would never play in Leicester again. Instead, I went to play my league snooker in Coventry and our side was very successful there. It was also another source of income for me to be added to the money I was making from playing at Osborne's, as there were always side bets to be made in the league matches. I played for Standard Triumph along with Greg Baxter, Brian Cakebread and two brothers, Dave and Reef Berry, travelling there every week. The standard of player was much higher than it was in Leicester, but we were a good team, each of us capable of making decent breaks and we had a lot of success there, winning the CIU championship for three successive years, a tournament which was probably the biggest around for a three-man team.

After winning that first title back in 1970 I got the chance to play against one the game's greats. A national exhibition tour had been set up by a brewery, featuring three-times world champion Fred Davis and Rex Williams. They would play nine frames against each other and then play against the local snooker champion in the particular area they were visiting. The tour also saw them play against the most promising player from the area, and as I'd become the national under-16 champion I was given the opportunity to play Fred at the working men's club in Evington, a district in east Leicester.

It was a very exciting day for me as I made my way to the club accompanied by my mum and dad. The travelling show with Davis and Williams featured a table, seating and scoreboard, and there were about 300 people packed into the hall as I stepped up to face Fred. I'd never played in front of such a big audience before. I had a light-brown suit on with a nice shirt and tie that my parents had got me and I have to say that, although I was a little bit nervous at the start, I soon settled into it and enjoyed myself.

I loved playing in front of an audience and I think I began to feed off the fact that I was out there, centre stage, with the great Fred Davis. You could say I was a bit flash, but I prefer to think of it as being confident and very comfortable. The whole environment suited me and suited my personality. Yes there was a bit of the showman in me, but I also felt as though playing snooker was something which came easily; it was a game I really enjoyed and was good at. I didn't make any stunning breaks, but at the same time I played well enough to beat Fred. He was a real gentleman, and I had my picture taken with him after the match. He was very complimentary about the way I'd performed and told me what a good player I was for my age. I think I smiled politely and thanked him, but inside I was bursting with pride and excitement. To have him tell me I was a good player was a huge thing and the whole evening was something I have never forgotten. It gave me a lot of satisfaction, and it was just the sort of thing a young player needs.

I was very much in love with the game and I can remember the thrill I got one day when I went to Manchester to watch John Spencer play in an exhibition match. I had tremendous respect for John, and think he was one of the truly great world champions the game has produced. I watched in complete awe as he made a 147 maximum break, and the way he played was truly inspirational. I wanted to be able to emulate him and the excitement his memorable performance generated that night among the 150 people crammed into a working men's club.

As well as winning national titles, my ability also later led to me becoming the youngest player to represent England at that time. It was a great honour and a really good experience to play for my country. There was no real money involved – we were just given expenses – but it was nice to stay in hotels and travel with the team. The amateur game still predominated in terms of the number of people playing it, and there were some good young, talented kids coming through – people like Tony Knowles and Joe Johnson, who were a bit younger than me, and John Virgo who was slightly older. To play for your country was a fabulous experience and I enjoyed every minute of it, including one weekend which started well but might have ended in disaster.

I became good friends with Mark Wildman during the course of playing internationals, and we would often have a laugh and a giggle whenever we were on duty for our country. Mark was a few years older than me and later went on to become become a professional snooker player as well as the chairman of the World Professional Billiards and Snooker Association, but back then he was more than happy to get involved in some harmless betting fun. We once had a £10 bet over whether the chairman of the amateur snooker board would take his glasses off during the course of a speech he was giving on the day of an international in Exeter. Mark reckoned he would take them off about halfway through, but despite touching the edge of his frames several times, the glasses stayed on, with the two of us in fits of laughter.

I was due to play in a tournament in Grimsby the next day and decided that in order to get there for my midday start time, I would drive to Leicester that same night, stay over, and then set off early the next morning for Grimsby. I was tired but set off hoping to reach Leicester in time to have a decent night's sleep. By the time I reached Birmingham I was beginning to really feel it and was desperately trying to stay awake. At one point I saw a huge lorry about 150 yards in front of me and I started to slow down. But I must have dropped off for a split second, and the next thing I knew I was just about to plough into the back of it. I jammed on my brakes and managed to slow down enough to stop me crunching into the back of him. If I hadn't woken up when I did I'm convinced I would have crashed and killed myself.

It was a big enough scare for me to want to pull over at the next available service station to give myself a chance to rest and get over the shock. I pulled in, put my seat back and quickly fell into a deep sleep. So deep, in fact, that the next thing I remember was sitting bolt upright with my eyes wide open in blind panic as my brain vividly replayed the brush with death I'd experienced. I finally made it to Leicester and then onto Grimsby the next day for the tournament final I was playing in. Grimsby was a hotbed for snooker in those days and it was quite common for a tournament to be played in various locations around the country before having the final, or final stages at Grimsby. These tournaments were taking place regularly, with people like John Virgo, Patsy Fagan (who would go on to win the 1977 UK Championship) and Dennis Taylor competing. I can't remember if I won that one, but I certainly did well in others that were staged.

With my reputation as a snooker player growing, I was beginning to earn some very decent money from the amateur game, so there was no rush to turn professional. I know that may sound strange, but the truth was that professional snooker was nothing like it is now. There were no huge tournaments in this country or around the globe back then. Of course, winning the World Championship was a tremendous achievement, but it didn't make you a rich man. The prize money for winning the World Championship in 1972 was £480, which was fine, but certainly not exceptional and it was a one-off event. I could earn more from money matches than I would in professional tournaments.

That year, I did come across a young player who had taken the plunge and turned professional and would become one of the game's greatest entertainers. He had reached the World Championship final, to be held at Selly Park British Legion in Birmingham. His name was Alex Higgins and he was just 22 years old. By this time I had come in to contact with a lot of the country's top players, and there was no doubt Alex fell into that category.

Leicester isn't too far away from where the venue for the final was and my mum and dad were happy to put him up at our house. It was something my mother got used to in the years that followed, because I would often turn up on her doorstep with snooker-playing friends from all over the world, people like Cliff Thorburn and Bill Werbeniuk from Canada and Jimmy Van Rensburg from South Africa. In fact, big Bill once turned up at my mum's place and ended up staying for a year and a half!

When Alex arrived at our house, he stood in front of my mum and held out a tiny case. "Do something with this for me," he told her. Inside he'd packed a dress suit and bow tie. She ended up ironing and pressing it for him so that it was wearable for the tournament. It was typical of Alex, and over the years he would often stay at our place.

My mum was as good as gold and would always fuss and look after whoever came to stay. She loved having them around and she loved watching snooker. On that first occasion, I was asked by his management company if I wanted to be Alex's right-hand man during the final. It would have meant driving him around and generally looking after him, but I declined. I was happy enough to get in some practice frames with him during his time with us, and I did get a bit of a kick out of the fact that at the end of the tournament, which Alex won by beating John Spencer in the final, I had been playing frames against the new world champion.

My own snooker playing was still very much based at Osborne's. There was some very good money to be made in the billiard halls because of all the betting that went on. Players would challenge each other, and there would always be side stakes on the outcome of the matches. You could bet on yourself and then there would also be your mates who might have travelled with you, who would also bet on the games. I could pick up £100 or £200 for some money matches, at a time when £200 was a pretty decent weekly wage. The existence of this world eventually made me decide to give up work and concentrate on my snooker full time.

I had enjoyed working at Norman & Underwood; it was a decent job and I must have been doing all right because I was eventually headhunted by another company called Edens, who wanted me to do the same sort of thing. Once again I had the freedom to be pretty much my own boss, and I also got a car with the job. It meant that I was able to fit my work around playing snooker, and I have to admit I began taking more and more time off to devote to my game. It got to the point where it really wasn't worth me carrying on with the job. Each weekend I could play in snooker matches that would make me perhaps £80 or even £100, which was certainly more than I was earning from my job at Edens.

In the end I went to see Barry Eden, who owned the company, and explained the situation. He was very good about it and could see I had already made my mind up. We remained friends and I know he followed my career closely in the years that followed. The decision meant that I was a professional player in the sense that I began to earn money from playing matches, but in terms of the way snooker was defined I was still very much an amateur player and there was still a lot for me to learn when it came to playing the game. I also got extra cash on occasions from betting on the horses and that part of my life continued to evolve alongside my snooker-playing.

The betting culture at Osborne's seemed to be second nature to so many of the people who played at the club. One of them was a character named 'Racing Raymond' Winterton. He had worked for his father, a bookmaker, at various tracks and then inherited his pitches. He was older than me by about ten years, but we got on very well and soon became great friends. He was a big guy who weighed more than 20 stone and he was very good fun to be with. Raymond knew that I liked betting on the horses and it wasn't long before I not only used the bookmakers next to Osborne's, but I was also placing bets at various race-courses after he invited me down to the track for a meeting one day. It was a whole new world and one I immediately took to.

I loved the atmosphere, enjoyed the whole experience and the buzz that it gave me. It was one thing putting a bet on in the bookies, but gambling at a track and then standing there as the horse I was backing ran its race felt so very different. The sights, the sounds and the people brought the whole thing to life. Although betting was at the heart of what I was there for, I also had a sense of being part of an occasion. To me, it was magical.

Many of the same people who would enjoy a day at the races also used to love watching me play snooker and having a gamble on the results of my matches. So Raymond, together with several other characters from the club, would regularly accompany me when I travelled to other parts of the country to compete against the best players their particular billiard hall had to offer. I would give all of my opponents a bit of a start and then we would have bets of £200, or £300 on me winning the match sometimes. It was always very profitable for us, and happily it went on for some years.

I had some great times doing this, and probably one of my most profitable destinations was Birmingham. There were eight or ten good players in the city – some of them had reached county standard – who would regularly play me. I used to love going there because no matter how many times I beat people, they would still call up and ask if I fancied a rematch.

I was never a horrible or arrogant winner and I think they liked me as a person, which may have been one of the reasons they asked me back so many times. I would go to Birmingham, play for four or five hours, clean up the money, before travelling back to Leicester. They would also come over to Osborne's and the same thing would happen. I always used to win, and over a period of quite a few years I probably took around £40,000 or £50,000 from them. For me, it was a licence to print money.

There was one guy who was called 'Bob the Butcher'. He ran his own billiard hall and was a very decent player. He could play one-handed and make breaks of 20, or 30, but I would give him a 40 points start per frame and still beat him. I would give other players a 14 or 21-point start just to entice them into playing me. I played one guy who used a half butt cue and gave him an 80 start. It was all good fun.

On one occasion about six of them came over from Birmingham to play me at Osborne's. They sat there waiting their turn on the table, one after the other. It was like a dentist's waiting room, I'd call one up, beat him and then move on to the next.

There was a very talented player from Birmingham called Steve James, who went on to reach number seven in the world rankings. In the early Eighties, I was always trying to offer little inducements for him to play me because I fancied my chances against him, but he kept on turning me down. It was all good-natured stuff and one day we came up with the idea of giving him a 70 start in a five-frame game, but all I had to do to win the match was win one of the frames. He must have thought he was on a winner and that 70 was just too much to give a player of his standard. But I knew that even against a really good player, I would at some stage during those five frames make a break of 100. I could have played Stephen Hendry when he was at his peak, offered to do the same, and been very confident of winning one of the frames. Sure enough, on this particular occasion Steve started well and won the first frame, but then I made a

138 break in the second and the match was over with me winning the wager.

It was all about giving myself an edge and then making sure I took advantage of it. I'm sure it also had a lot to do with the natural gambling instinct I had in me. In my own mind I was working out the odds and I knew that although the bet sounded good to my opponent, the odds favoured me.

I used to love playing for money and never had any real fear when it came to pitting my snooker wits against an opponent for cash. My problems came later on when I had become a professional, because despite all of my natural talent I was often mentally fragile during the course of a tournament and lost matches against people I should have beaten easily. I'm convinced that if I'd been playing those same people for money in a billiard hall more often than not I would have won.

It was never a case of the crowds getting to me; I could handle that and always loved an audience. It was just a case of me not being able to focus sufficiently and failing to be single-minded enough to push myself over that finish line in big tournaments. It's something I will always regret, and it was never an easy thing to live with when it happened. I'd lie awake in my hotel room sometimes going over and over the match I had lost that day, trying to work out exactly what had gone wrong. More often than not the conclusion I came to was not how well my opponent had played, but how poorly I had performed.

I don't know whether I lost concentration or whether I was just mentally weak, but it happened too often for it just to be misfortune. And yet, let me loose on a one-off money match in a billiard hall and I invariably came up with the goods. A great example of this came years after my Osborne's days when I had left the amateur game behind and become a professional. I was playing in the prestigious Masters tournament down in London and was contacted by a character known as 'Jack the Aussie' who, unsurprisingly, was from Australia. He had made his money over there through some business or other and fancied himself as a bit of a snooker player, which he most certainly wasn't. I knew of Jack because I'd heard he'd been playing other people for money. I also heard that he turned up for these games carrying two bags. One was a paper bag which was full of the money he was going to bet with, and the other was a plastic carrier bag that contained a pair of socks. Believe it or not, he would actually change his socks halfway through a match!

To say he was a bit eccentric would be putting it mildly, but he loved to play and I was happy to oblige. I gave him a start of 80 every frame and there was no time limit on the match itself. All I wanted to make sure I did was empty his paper bag of cash. I began the match thinking there was about £15,000 in it, but it soon became apparent that there was quite a bit more. We started at about 2pm one afternoon and it took me about 24 hours before I finally got all the dough off of him. It was totally exhausting. If you give someone an 80 start over five frames, it's no problem because your mind is clear, but to play all day long when you have to score 100 points every frame is a very different matter. I knew he couldn't make 20, but he could play safety snooker. I realised that I would get four or five opportunities each frame where I would get the chance to make an 80 break and I knew that when they came along I had to capitalise on the situation, but it was the length of the match which proved to be exhausting. I eventually got into my car after beating him and taking around £20,000 in the process. It had been tough both physically and mentally, but I came through and finished the job I had started. I got behind the wheel to begin my drive home but after driving a couple of miles I had to give up, because I was totally gone. I had to let a friend of mine take over the driving while I had a sleep on the back seat, and I didn't wake up again until we got back to Leicester.

The point of all of this is that I stuck in there and made sure I won. However, that wasn't the case during countless tournaments.

I must have played around 100 matches at Osborne's where there was money on the outcome, and the only person ever to beat me there was Patsy Fagan, a renowned money player in his prime. I loved playing snooker and I loved the whole gambling social scene that was prevalent there. I was hooked.

Snooker and horse racing had become my twin obsessions in life. The former helped to make me a lot of money, the latter ensured an awful lot of it was wasted.

CHAPTER FIVE

TAKING A PUNT

It is very difficult to fully convey to a non-gambler the feeling I got when I first stood in that bookmakers next to Osborne's and cheered on the horse I had backed. I can't tell you what the horse was called or what price it was, I can't even tell you how much I won, but I can tell you about the sheer rush of adrenalin I got from picking a winner. It must sound very strange to a lot of people, but it was an absolutely wonderful feeling. It wasn't just about winning, it was knowing that I had taken a gamble and it had paid off. I had backed my judgement and instinct and come out on top, beaten the system.

Most addicted gamblers will tell you that in many ways the money, or rather the amount you bet, doesn't matter, it's all about the thrill betting gives you. I know that ultimately money does begin to matter, particularly when you dig the sort of hole I did later on in my life, when I had to go 'on the chase' in the hope of getting the money I needed to get me out of the awful financial situation I found myself in. But back in the days when I was enjoying playing snooker and the social scene at Osborne's, having a bet on the horses came as naturally as potting a red. Once I progressed from placing my bets in the bookies to actually going to the track, there was really no way back for me.

I loved every minute and going along with Raymond and some of our pals made it all the more enjoyable. It was great watching Raymond in action at all the various tracks around Britain putting all the experience he'd gained over the years into action, and it wasn't long before I got more involved in the proceedings when I learned how to tick-tack (the sign language with which bookmakers on the racing course communicate). I took to it straight away and really enjoyed being a part of the action. In the years that followed I had many fantastic times at tracks with Raymond, and used to love going to the really big meetings during the course of a year. We would pack up and go away for days, staying at lovely hotels, eating great meals and generally having a lot of fun. Going to the Cheltenham Festival, the Derby at Epsom, Royal Ascot or Glorious Goodwood was wonderful. They were all great occasions and I would eagerly look forward to them each year, knowing that not only was there the chance to have a bet and make some money, but also that the trips provided great entertainment.

I wasn't the sort of person who blindly had a bet on a horse just because I liked its name. Like Greg Baxter at Osborne's, I studied form and the more I got involved in the racing world, the more I came into contact with professional gamblers who helped to expand my knowledge. Betting was their livelihood and in order to be successful at it you not only had to know what you were doing, you also had to have a whole network of people you rely on to give you tips and the right kind of advice. Knowing something about the individual horses and different races was the 'edge' I came to rely on more and more over the years that followed. I always tried to place a bet knowing I had good information about the horse. I'm not saying this meant that I had a winning formula, far from it, but I never just took a punt on a race. There was always some method, even if ultimately my gambling resulted in the financial madness I later found myself in.

There was one guy we knew who was known as 'Ginger Steve' and he was a very good judge with extremely good connections in the game. He was like lots of people in horse racing who had various 'ins' with characters connected with the sport. By an 'in' I mean having a worthwhile connection with somebody who is on the inside of racing and can pass on useful information. It's been going on for years and it will never change. Bookmakers will know people in the racing yards where horses are kept and trained, whether it's somebody like the head lad of the stable or the trainer. People have knowledge of what is going on with a horse, how it's running, whether it's carrying an injury and just generally what the feeling is about it around the yard, and that knowledge can be very valuable when it comes to making a bet. There is never any certainty that this information will guarantee you a winner, but it's certainly good to have it when you make your choice. I've had some great tips over the years and they have paid off handsomely; by the same token I have been convinced that a particular horse would do well because of what I have been told, only to lose heavily and regret ever putting the bet on in the first place.

When I look back now and think of all the races I've been to and the bets that I've had during my lifetime, I have come to the conclusion that I was never a lucky gambler. I've had some terrible results many years ago that should have proved to me once and for all that this was the case, but once you become a gambler you tend to forget, or rather, gloss over the bad times because the very nature of what you are means that you think you are always just one bet away from having a winner.

Stuttering Vic, one of my pals from those days back in Leicester, always set out with the intention of trying to make £100 from having a bet. For instance, he might go dog racing and have £100 on the favourite at events which, if it came home first, would give him the £100 win on his bet that he wanted. The trouble with Vic was that quite often the dog or horse that he had his money on would not win, so that would mean he would up his stakes in the next race to £200 in order to try and win £100. This could go on and on with Vic still trying to get that elusive £100. Sometimes he would end up spending £1,000 just to win £100!

He was a lovely guy and I remember him asking me in all seriousness once, "Wh. . ..wh. . ...wh. . ..why do you ca. . .ca. . ..ca. . ...call m. . .m. . .me Stuttering?"

I just looked at him, shook my head, smiled and asked, "Why do you think?"

Just like all of my other friends from those days, Vic was a real character and I suppose the common ingredient for all of us, apart from our love of gambling, was the fact that we all enjoyed each other's company and had such a great laugh together. Often it was the behavior of one of our group that made us all giggle. For example, the Red Faced Man from Braunston was about 40 years old, but still lived with his mum. He loved to hang out with all the other guys and enjoyed having a drink in the evenings, but despite his age he used to have this understanding with his mother that he would be home by 11pm. If it was 11.10pm and he hadn't arrived home, his mum would phone the police. She'd tell them she was worried about her son because he was missing. The local police would listen sympathetically and start to take details of her son before asking how old he was. They were clearly under the impression that she was talking about someone who was about ten, so you can imagine their reaction when they found out he was 40, had been out drinking with his mates and was only 10 minutes late!

As well as having a laugh there was a serious side to what a lot of these guys did as well. At least two of them were thieves and then there were others like Traffic Lights, who was a serious gambler. He was known as Traffic Lights because when he had a bet he would change colour. At the race track or in the bookies when he was cheering on the horse he'd backed, Traffic Lights' face would turn bright red, but as soon as the race was over, whether he'd won or lost, his face would go back to its natural white colour. He was a very clever guy and he earned a fortune by discovering a winning 'edge' in an entirely different sport.

His success came on the golf course – not as a player,

but as a punter. He was the first person to work out that you could win money from betting on the possibility of someone getting a hole-in-one. If you were to have asked most people at that time what they thought the odds were of a hole-in-one being achieved during the course of a tournament, they would have expected them to be pretty big. Most bookmakers would have given you odds of about 33/1, but in fact the right odds would have been even money because it happens more often than you might think, and that's where Traffic Lights made a killing. He and some of his pals would go all around the country laying small bets of £10 or £20 for a hole-in-one happening at various tournaments. The bets didn't raise any suspicion because they were quite small, but when you're getting paid out at 33/1 and there have been lots of bets placed, you can soon see how they all mounted up. He made an awful lot of money – and I'm talking hundreds of thousands of pounds – simply because he had worked out how to take advantage of the wrong odds. Obviously he had a limited period in which to make money on the bets, because the bookies soon realised what the correct odds should be. I think it was a question of perception because a hole-in-one is not something that happens every day. But that didn't matter, it just had to happen often enough for Traffic Lights to make his money, which was exactly what he did. He has since become one of the most respected tipsters around, with punters seeking out his views on a regular basis.

Having the intelligence to work something like that out and then to capitalise from it obviously has its rewards, but it also shows the difference between someone whose mind is tuned in to gambling and the possibilities open to them, rather than the ordinary guy in the street. Knowing about odds can make all the difference. Another example is the odds that used to be offered on a 147 break in snooker. Achieving a maximum is still an outside bet today, but in years gone by you could probably have got something like 50/1 on the chance of it happening, now it's more like 9/4 or 2/1. People are now more aware of the fact that there is the possibility of it occurring. Perception can have a big say it what people think their chances of winning are. Another example would be to ask someone what they thought the odds would be of producing a pair of identical cards from two different packs, if they were turning over one card from each pack at the same time. I suspect most people would come up with odds of 500/1 because you're talking about 52 cards in one pack and 52 in the other, but it's actually even money that it will happen, and having an understanding of things like that and being able to successfully calculate odds was something I found really interesting when I worked with Racing Raymond on his pitches at various tracks.

Going to the races was a real rush for me from day one. I loved it and wanted to make sure I stayed a part of it, because I enjoyed the whole thing so much. As well as tick-tacking, I also used to clerk for Raymond and have a share of the book, which, again, I found really enjoyable. I think I've always had a mathematical brain and was very good at figures from an early age. This might sound a bit bizarre considering the way I got into trouble financially in later years, but my problems sprang from the fact that I simply never paid enough attention to the way I handled money, not to the fact that I couldn't add up. I suppose that having a mathematical brain is something that most snooker players have anyway. A big part of the game is about calculating things in your head as you're playing, the points on the table and the angles you play your shots at. It's probably a natural way of thinking for many players, and I also think that the gambling element of my character had a lot to do with the way I played the game and went about things. Perhaps I took risks when I should have played safe, simply because I liked the idea of taking a chance on a shot, believing I had the ability to pull off what I was trying to do. A lot of the time that worked for me and, certainly in the early part of my snooker-playing days, I think my confidence in my own ability won me a lot of matches. When I was at Osborne's playing for money I didn't have any fear, I just went for it and had enough belief to make sure I came through.

I was still doing well with my snooker and making very decent money from it. I can't honestly tell you whether I had great success at the track, but I do know that I enjoyed the whole experience. As long as I was making money at the snooker table and there was a ready supply of cash, it allowed me to indulge in my other passion which was the horses, so all was well. My parents and brothers certainly had no idea about my gambling because from the age of about 16 I led a pretty independent life, even though I was still based at home.

In the years which followed, the only thing which really changed was the amount of money that came in and went out. Apart from that, the process was pretty much the same: I loved playing snooker, I got money from it; I loved having a bet on the horses and I spent money on it.

I never once sat down to analyse or plan for the future. I was having a good time and enjoying myself, so what was there to worry about? It may sound a bit reckless, but I was young, I had a talent for a sport that enabled me to earn money from it even though I wasn't a professional and I was having a great time with a lot of mates who were into the same things as me. They might not have been as good at snooker, but they were all part of the scene at Osborne's and for whatever reason I fitted in well there and felt very much at home too.

Professional snooker might not have been the money-making exercise it became in the 1980s, but the sport did start to be seen more regularly on our television screens, and that was really due to a programme called *Pot Black* which had so much to do with making snooker the game it later became to the viewing public. The format was very simple: it was a half-hour programme in which only a single frame was played. It was first aired in 1969 and became very popular at the start of the next decade, not least because people were beginning to buy colour televisions. It also did much to counter snooker's seedy public image. If you asked someone in 1970 what their image of snooker was, it would probably be of a game played by shady characters in dark, smoky halls or in a pub somewhere in the backstreets of a city – and they wouldn't have been far wrong. But *Pot Black* came along and dressed the whole thing up nicely, giving snooker a bit of a makeover in the process. The players looked wholesome and wore nice suits, instead of appearing to be the sort of characters who might want to try and sell you some dodgy goods that had fallen off the back of a lorry. The players involved were the sort of people the public had no problem taking to. The game itself was placed into a neatly packaged format, and the fact that it only took up half an hour added to its appeal and popularity.

Like anyone else who played the game, I was an avid viewer and once actually got the chance to go and see the programme being recorded. Becoming *Pot Black* champion opened up some great opportunities for the winner, because you were virtually guaranteed about ten years of lucrative exhibition matches as a result, as well as having your profile lifted because of the fact that a national television audience tuned in to watch proceedings. Graham Miles won it in both 1974 and 1975 and became something of a star. It was seen as far more important back then to be *Pot Black* champion than the world champion, simply because of the exposure the programme gave you.

Graham was the player I was lucky enough to see in action when I went to watch the show being recorded in 1973. The words 'lucky' and 'recorded' are particularly significant in recalling what happened to me some months later. I was wandering around the Isle of Wight in the summer of 1974, having gone there to visit a girlfriend I had at the time. I was strolling down the street one morning and came face to face with a sign in the window of a bookmakers shop which made me stand and stare in disbelief. It gave the odds for the *Pot Black* programme which was due to be screened that night, offering Miles at 20/1.

Now having an 'in' when you have a bet can be very important, as I have already said, but having the sort of inside knowledge I had of this particular event was pretty much unheard of. I just knew Graham Miles would come out on top. In fact, I was absolutely sure he would for one very simple reason: I had seen him win the very same tournament several months ago when I'd gone to watch the programme being made!

The bookies were offering odds on something that had already taken place, and after getting over the initial shock of seeing that sign, I very quickly realised that this was the betting equivalent of manna from heaven, a once-in-a-lifetime chance. It's incredible to think of it in this day and age when we can switch on our television sets and watch hundreds of channels, where news is instantaneous and the internet has become so much part of our lives, but in those days there were just three television channels, programme-making was nothing like it is today. It obviously never occurred to the bookies that this was a recorded show.

I was aware I had to be careful not to raise suspicion if I was going to make the sort of financial killing which an opportunity like this gave me. It was no good going into the bookies and lumping on a huge bet, so I had to place small bets, not all of them on Graham, but some on the other possible winners, like Ray Reardon and Fred Davis, who were also part of the whole programme. I'd have £5 on Ray and then £10 on Fred, before putting £30 or £40 on Graham. I repeated this quite a few times and pretended I was putting a bet on for my dad or a mate. The outcome was that I ended up winning about £500 or

£600, which was an absolute fortune at the time, and would be the equivalent of thousands of pounds today. On a moral level I suppose you could say it wasn't the best thing to do, but it was just too good an extraordinary opportunity to pass up.

I had a lot to thank the programme for on that occasion, and *Pot Black* was to play a pivotal role in my life a couple of years later, when I was invited to actually take part in it. I was jogging along nicely at the time and was quite happy with the way things were going. I was still only 21 years old, I was making decent money from playing on the amateur circuit, with all the wagers and side betting that took place in the billiard halls, pubs and clubs and there just wasn't really the need to become a professional. I was one of the best amateur players around. I was still going to the race courses with Raymond and the rest of the lads from Osborne's, so I had a pretty carefree existence. Life was all about having fun and that suited me perfectly, but it didn't mean I wasn't ambitious or without ego. Not in a horrible way, but I was certainly confident in my own ability as a snooker player and when I'd gone to watch the programme being recorded, I honestly felt I had nothing to fear from the players I watched. Don't get me wrong, a player like Ray Reardon was superb and one of the best the game has ever had, I just had an honest belief that I wouldn't feel out of place in the company of people like Graham Miles and some of his contemporaries.

I got my chance to prove just that thanks to the wonderful Ted Lowe, the snooker commentator whose voice became such a part of the sport on television. His distinctive delivery earned him the nickname of 'Whispering Ted' because of his low rumbling voice which was so reminiscent of John Arlott, a commentator who gave a lovely warm feel to any cricket match he was working on. It's true to say that Ted changed my life in 1975 when he asked me to take part in *Pot Black*, because in order to do so I had to relinquish my amateur status and become a professional snooker player at the age of 21. It was the same year I had reached the final of the English Amateur Championships, losing to 11-6 to Sid Hood. There was no doubt that my name was becoming well known within the amateur game, but back then, with the exception of Alex Higgins, no one of my age became a snooker professional. Other than Alex, the youngest of them were probably in their late twenties or early thirties. It was nothing like it is today when you get kids in their teens turning professional and able to hold their own against the established pros straight away. It was a very different world, and there was no doubt that when I entered it I was a bit of a novelty.

I had to go to the BBC's Pebble Mill studios to play in *Pot Black* and I wasn't exactly a shrinking violet when I turned up at the place. I was pretty full of myself. I had cards printed saying that I was the world's youngest professional and they also listed the titles I had won as an amateur. I also had a lovely leather cue case with my initials on it. Ted had really put himself out on my behalf to get me on the programme, and looking back now I know I had an awful lot to thank him for. It was a great shame when I heard about his death in spring 2011. Ironically, I was at the World Championships at the Crucible in Sheffield, commentating for the BBC, so in a way I was following in his footsteps, although there will never be another Ted Lowe. When the news of his passing came through, I think everyone in the snooker world felt a loss, but at the same time it was lovely that so many of us who knew him had our own very personal memories of the great man.

I have to admit I didn't quite cover myself in glory during my debut on *Pot Black*. Despite being pretty confident in my own ability, once I got there and realised I was actually rubbing shoulders with the same players I had avidly watched on the box along with many other viewers, I began to feel less certain about myself. The other thing which didn't help was that two of my heroes, John Spencer and Ray Reardon, were among the players taking part. We recorded for five days and the programmes of matches we played were going to be part of a series to be shown later in the following summer. The frames were meant to be short and sharp affairs, to make sure they retained the interest of the viewing public when the programmes were eventually broadcast. That format suited my game because I was a naturally quick player who never liked to linger over his shots, but although I won a few frames, I didn't make it to the semi-finals. Instead I had to make do with a £500 fee for taking part as I started out in my professional career.

What I quickly came to realise was the kind of power a popular programme like *Pot Black* had. From being a pretty anonymous bloke with the ability to pot snooker balls in billiard halls around the country, the exposure I got from going on the programme opened up a new and lucrative avenue of the game for me. I was suddenly able to command high fees for playing exhibition matches. They started at about £50 or £100 and quickly rose to the £250 and £300 level, which was pretty decent money in the late 1970s and the money got considerably better in the Eighties.

The basic format of an exhibition didn't really change too much. If it was at a club they would surround a table with some tiered seating and then you would play a frame each against their seven best players. If it was in a leisure centre in the Eighties there would be a bigger crowd and it would often involve me playing against another professional. On one occasion I remember going to a snooker club in Balham, South London, along with Patsy Fagan. They asked us to play against a couple of their youngsters, and so we gave them a 21 start in matches that were played over five frames. One of the kids was only about 14 and the other must have been just a few years older. Both Patsy and I ended up getting beaten 3-1. The 14-year-old turned out to be Jimmy White and the other kid was Tony Meo. It was a good job we'd given them the 21 start, because at least it gave us a way of saving a bit of face! But it was obvious that the pair of them had real talent, as was proven in the years which followed.

I also got some great publicity soon after the filming for the *Pot Black* programme had taken place. I did a photo shoot which was later featured in the *Radio Times*, with a picture of me on the front cover of the magazine. It was great for the ego but at the same time it had a very practical side to it as well, because suddenly I began to get recognised and my profile as a professional snooker player rose considerably.

My intention was to move up the ranking and make as much money from the game as I could. Unfortunately I was hardly an overnight success and my progress as a professional was slow. I found it hard going, and looking back now I realise I probably turned professional too early. It was to be a tough five years before I made my big breakthrough with a tournament win but, although it was often difficult in terms of competitive success, I was still having a wonderful time.

Apart from my snooker, horse racing was as important as ever in my life. In fact, I'd become more and more infatuated with it as the years went by. I still went to the courses with Raymond and although I had become better known because of snooker and had appeared on television, it didn't stop me working with him until sometime later when my face became too well known to carry on ticktacking. My love of horse racing and betting showed no sign of easing up. I got a great buzz from betting. The anticipation and excitement that went with it was just incredible, win or lose. I didn't realise just how heavily I was getting into it because everyone I closely associated with had a bet. It was part of all our lives – in fact, it was our way of life and I was enjoying it more and more.

CHAPTER SIX

MR MAXIMUM

It was exciting being a professional snooker player, but the inconsistency I displayed was in marked contrast to my days as a carefree amateur who was happy to challenge anyone for a side wager on the match. Put me up against another player, ask me to stake my own money against theirs, and the most likely outcome would be a win for me. It wouldn't have mattered if I was playing in my own backyard, or travelling around the country, but playing in tournaments somehow seemed different.

I was playing in a new environment to the one I had become accustomed to and perhaps that had something to do with it, even though it shouldn't really have mattered when the sport is your profession. The game might have been the same, but I was probably out of my comfort zone and that showed in my play. I was always the sort of player who did things instinctively and the game had always come easily to me. I was happy sticking to the same sort of training regime I'd always had as an amateur, which had the added benefit of allowing me plenty of time to pursue my gambling interest.

Certainly, when I was playing well I could go into a match feeling confident after not putting in the sort of hours lots of other players might have. It was when I wasn't playing too well that I felt I needed to practise more. When that was the case, I would practise between 10am and midday, before having a bit of lunch and maybe going to the bookies. I'd then go back and practise for perhaps an hour and a half before another break and then have a couple of hours in the evening. Rather than solo practice, I used to like playing against someone if that was possible and I always focused on building breaks.

The other factor which tended to curtail my practice was that I was often out playing exhibition matches, and that meant I had to do a lot of travelling. This never really bothered me because a couple of hours' practice per day was usually alright for me. When it came to the big tournaments, I would put aside the week before to practise every day and I never used to have a bet at all. Looking back now, I realise that I should have devoted a month to it and, who knows, maybe that would have made a difference to me winning more of the big ones.

Raymond and the rest of the lads were always great supporters when it came to tournaments, and they would follow me around the country hoping I would win matches and at the same time they had bets on the outcome of the games I was involved in. They were very loyal and were always there to tell me it wasn't really my fault if I lost a match. I was also very good at making excuses for myself if things didn't quite work out, and this kind of mental attitude became a common theme throughout my playing days. I suppose I was never quite prepared to take full responsibility for my actions if things didn't work out the way I had hoped. I wasn't honest enough with myself and, although it was great of all the lads from Osborne's to follow me around, I have to admit they were never honest enough with me either. They gave me bags of encouragement and never found fault, even if they'd lost money on me, but I think what was needed from a very early stage in my professional career was a dose of reality.

I never really had one person in my corner spelling it out the way it was. Steve Davis did, he had his manager Barry Hearn, and I think their partnership worked perfectly. I'm sure that if things went badly and he lost a match, Barry would be the first one to tell him he was rubbish and highlight what had gone wrong. When you're involved in such a solitary game as snooker I think you need to have a person like that to talk to and confide in.

I also have to say that Steve was a very different sort of character to me. He was much more focused and dedicated than I ever was. In the days when players just went about their business in their own sweet way, Steve was ahead of his time in his approach to how he played his snooker, making sure he was mentally strong and prepared for tournament play. Even during a match I would often see him focusing on a particular object around the arena he was playing in, and he would stare at it, seemingly blocking all other thoughts out of his head. I don't know exactly what mental process he was going through, but I do know that it worked for him, and that sort of toughness, allied to his skill as a player, served him so well at his peak and it also helped him prolong his playing career at the top level way past most of his contemporaries.

I had a bunch of mates who were wonderfully supportive but who would never bring me down to earth with the kind of harsh criticism that my game sometimes deserved. What I did have was probably the best following on the professional snooker circuit, which was great for me at the time and I enjoyed having them around. In many ways it was just a continuation of what had happened throughout my time at Osborne's. Sadly, though, my association with the club ended following an argument over something pretty trivial.

The Osbornes had always made me feel really at home whenever I was at the club, and I always looked upon Ernie Osborne as a second father. If ever I needed a few bob he would let me have some until I could pay him back. If I wanted a cup of tea or a Mars bar, I would just help myself and put the money behind the counter – everything was very relaxed and informal. One day I was in the club and the phone began to ring in the office. There was nobody near to answer it, so I went in and did just that. It was something I'd done before when Mr and Mrs O were there, but on this particular occasion they weren't around. Their son, Barry, was though, and he came charging over and started having a real go at me.

"You're not supposed to be in the office," he shouted.

"I've always gone in the office and there's never been a problem," I told him but he was having none of it.

"Don't you ever come in this office again!" he screamed.

I was so shocked that I didn't really have a reply. I just

76

found the whole incident really upsetting and I walked out of the place in a bit of a daze. I couldn't believe what had happened. I'd felt so comfortable throughout my time at the club and now, because of a stupid little incident, I felt like a stranger. Worse still, Barry had made it sound like I'd done something terrible, even though all I'd tried to do was answer the phone just as I had done countless other times before. When he refused to apologise to me for the incident, that was it, I never went back.

It was a shame because the place had meant so much to me. I had first walked through its doors as a kid, and in many ways I'd learned my trade there, winning all of those national titles along the way. I'd had wonderful times and made great friends, including the Osbornes themselves.

I still have great memories of the place and the people I met there, even though I'm sure that, indirectly, my exposure to the sort of culture which existed in the club helped fuel my betting instincts. It might be nice to think that if I hadn't gone to Osborne's my gambling addiction might never have started, but I'm not sure that is the case. I know it didn't help, but it was just a stage in my life, and I'm sure the urge to gamble would have manifested itself in another way and in another place if I hadn't gone there. Lots of people are exposed to the temptations of gambling but never succumb, or at least not to the extent I did. It's really all about me and what I am. I know that now, but I was unaware of such things then. Life was very simple as far as I was concerned, and it was just up to me to go on and try to live it to the full.

Betting was as much part of my life as having something to eat and drink. It never once seemed a strange thing to do. I never felt guilty about it or tried to hide it from anyone. The fact that my family probably never knew too much about what I was doing was because I just got on with my own life, and as far as they were concerned I was doing fine.

I don't think betting was in the blood, even though my dad would like to go to the races sometimes. He'd have the odd £50 bet and he also got involved with owning a horse called Lana's Secret later on in his life, but certainly was never into gambling in the way that I was. Malcolm might have had the occasional flutter on a big race or snooker match, but I can't ever recall my mum or Robert betting at all. So when it came to gambling I think I was pretty much a one-off in my family.

The struggle to make a real impact on the professional circuit continued for some years, and I have no doubt that the main reason for it was my lack of mental strength, and that in turn led to inconsistency. It was something I knew was part of my make-up and I even tried going to a hypnotist in order to get on top of the problem, but he could never quite get me to go 'under' and there weren't sports psychologists around as there are today. Gambling might have contributed to my concentration, or rather a lack of it, during matches in the latter part of my career, when my mind might have wandered, but before that it was not being able to deal with some of the key points in matches which was often so frustrating.

I knew I had ability, that was never in question, and I

seemed to be able to turn it on against the top players because my concentration was good when I knew I had to be at my best to win. But against lesser players I would sometimes drift in and out of a game, allowing my opponent to get back into a match or take advantage of my mental lapses. I'd make 90 or 100 breaks in some games and then in others I wouldn't be able to get past 20, which was ridiculous. This type of thing tended to manifest itself more in the best-of-nine-frame matches, whereas in tournaments like the UK and World Championships where the matches were longer, I tended to feel more comfortable because there wasn't the pressure to get over the winning line as quickly. It meant I was more able to deal with the loss of a frame because there were usually plenty more to come.

One of my problems was that I wasn't able to clear the doubts in my head if I lost a frame. Instead of just putting it to one side and getting on with the next frame, I would go to the table still thinking about what had happened and wondering if I was going to mess things up again. I also liked to play quickly and never hung around when I was potting balls, which was fine when I was in action, but snooker also involves you having to stay mentally strong and focused when you are not at the table. You often have to sit there watching your opponent hit balls into the pockets as he starts to score, and obviously you have to keep thinking and be ready to go to the table when your chance comes. If you start to drift and let your mind wander, as I often did, then it can certainly affect your game.

It was frustrating, particularly as I was making centuries and maximum 147 breaks in practice, but transferring that sort of form to tournaments proved difficult for me. I still made decent money, though, because I was doing well on the exhibition circuit, where I could have played virtually every night if I'd had the time, and I was able to have a very good lifestyle. The buzz of betting on the horses was still a big part of my life and, although I often found the snooker frustrating, I still had a lot of belief in my own ability and knew that if I got everything together I was capable of beating anyone and winning tournaments.

I was becoming better known because of my snooker playing and got quite a lot of publicity locally, particularly after I gave the press something a bit more worthwhile to write about when I won the Pontins Spring Open in 1980, beating Cliff Wilson 7-3 in the final.

It had taken me five years to win my first tournament and, while I never had any doubts about my ability during those barren years, there's no doubt that coming to terms with the professional game took me longer than I had thought it would. I had started out confident that I could make the switch and ease my way up the rankings, but I was very much the junior member of the profession and things didn't come as easily as I thought they would. Getting that first win was a relief, and it was also a nice boost to my confidence.

Looking back on that period in my life, I can now see it was part of a learning curve for me. Until then everything had come easily, and I was a bit precocious when it came to my snooker. I did a lot in a short space of time as a teenager and thought that would be repeated in my twenties, but it wasn't to be and I think I had to mature as a player before I started to feel more comfortable with professional tournament play.

Having experienced a place like Osborne's and known what it had done for me as a player, I knew there was a big market for snooker in the Leicester area, and providing a modern set-up where people could go to play and socialise was something the area cried out for. There really weren't many snooker centres in this country at the time, but one had opened in Leeds during the late 1970s and done very well, which convinced me a similar sort of thing would work in Leicester. So I decided to do something about it by opening a club of my own. I wasn't exactly awash with money at the time and the whole project only got off the ground because of a lot of hard work and effort, not just from me but also from my partners in the venture, namely Mum and my brothers Malcolm and Robert. It was very much a family affair, although my dad had nothing to do with it. By this time my parents had split up and gone their separate ways, with dad continuing as the landlord of The Falcon pub. Malcolm gave up his job with a shoe company and Robert stopped working as a butcher in order to concentrate on our new business venture which we were going to call the Willie Thorne Snooker Centre.

We had to get the money together and plan exactly what it was going to look like before we eventually opened in the early 1980s. Once I'd made the decision to open a club we had to find suitable premises. We looked at an old office block and an old church before we finally came across exactly what we were looking for, even though it was rather unexpected. Somebody had told me to go and have a look at a building in Charles Street, Leicester. It had been an old rent and rates office, so at first I thought it wouldn't be right for a snooker club, but once I'd seen it I knew I couldn't have been more wrong. It was absolutely perfect, with wood-paneled walls which really added to the atmosphere of the place. It also had a ready-made cellar which had actually been used as a safe room, but because it had 18-inch blue brick walls with reinforced metal, it was perfect for storing beer in. We had ten tables in one room, another eight in an annex on the same floor, and then upstairs there was room for another ten tables. We had a bar/restaurant area and then another little section where I had my own snooker table with a picture of me on the wall and several other shots of the club at various stages of its development before we finally opened up to the public. My table was always covered if I wasn't playing on it, and we used to have the cloth changed about every three months. And I was never short of high-quality practice partners. Over the years, alongside the pictures of me, many photographs would be added of other professional snooker players who came to play there.

It was really my mum and two brothers who ran the club, with me taking a back seat, simply because I was not around that often. And from the very first days it was clear our optimism was well-founded and there was an immediate demand for what we offered. It wasn't just about snooker, although of course that was at the core of the place, but it was also a very sociable club, with a bar area and restaurant where mum's home cooking went down a treat. We did a roaring trade when it came to meals, and my mother was regularly cooking for more than 100 people at lunchtimes during peak periods like Christmas. Lots of the people who I'd known at Osborne's joined the club and clearly enjoyed having another place to play their snooker. It was great from my point of view as well because I had a first-class venue where I could practise any time I wanted to.

Previously, when I used to play at lunchtimes in Osborne's, there would often be quite a lot of people gathered round to watch me. Word had got out that I was a kid with a bit of talent for the game. I was making breaks of 80 and 100 even then, and I think a lot of the older players were fascinated by it. Once they saw I was able to do it on a regular basis, I think my games became something of an attraction at the club. I didn't mind this one bit and always loved having an audience. Two of the guys who were part of that audience were a father and son who owned a greengrocer's stall in the nearby market. They would pop in at lunchtimes or after work and, as well as watching me, they also used to like playing a game on the snooker table called 'Golf'. It involved using the six snooker pockets as holes and going from one to the other as you potted balls into them. I became quite friendly with the son, whose name was Barry, and when he found out that I liked playing cards he asked me around to his house one evening for a game. It soon developed into a pretty regular thing with me popping over most weeks for a game. Barry had a son who was about six years younger than me and was heavily into football.

At the time he was in the juniors at Leicester City but it wasn't just football that he was interested in, and I soon discovered that he was keen on most sports. Barry asked me if it was alright for his son to come down and watch me play, which he did. He also offered to have a game with me, and it was clear he had some talent for the game. It wasn't too long before his son had made his debut for Leicester, and by the time we opened the Snooker Centre he was making it as a striker. It didn't surprise me because I knew he was a talented footballer and a natural sportsman. We had become good friends despite the age difference and took a real interest in each other's careers as each of us became local personalities in Leicester. I was the snooker player trying to make a name for myself in the professional game, and he was the young footballer turning in impressive performances for City. I like to think I went on to do reasonably well and have a good career, and I'm sure you'll agree that Barry Lineker's son, Gary, did alright too!

I'm happy to say that the friendship we struck up all of those years ago remains to this day, and we certainly had some great times together back in the 1980s when he was a local hero playing for Leicester.

He was a good snooker player and would be happy to help me practise when he'd finished training for the day with City. He loved the game and was determined to get better at it, a trait he has shown throughout his life with whatever he has thrown himself into. Gary was naturally gifted when it came to sport involving a bat or ball, and that came across from a very early stage after we'd first met.

His enthusiasm for the game was very apparent and once my Snooker Centre opened he would be in the club to practise with me from early afternoon until 7pm or 8pm some days. Quite often he would play for five or six hours a day, and he was as serious about his snooker as he was about his football career. In fact, most days I would have to say that he practised more than me. I only used to be on the table for two or three hours, but you had to drag Gary off it!

When we played matches I would give him a 70 start and we would play the best of five frames. Although he was a very good player, like all sports, there is a difference between a talented amateur and a professional. After all, there's a reason for you being able to compete at the highest level of any game, and that is because you have that little bit extra that sets you apart. It would certainly have been the case with Gary and someone who was a really good amateur or non-league footballer and it was the same with me and him, but it certainly didn't mean he was a pushover and his determination to try and improve all the time was always a very impressive part of his character.

I used to love break-building against Gary, and he was on the wrong end of quite a few 147s during the time we played against each other, in fact, more than most players would experience in a lifetime. I used to love making a 147, and the reason I've never actually had a snooker table in my home is because I always wanted people to watch me do it. That was probably something to do with the way I felt after seeing John Spencer make that maximum. The thrill of seeing him build that break and then watching the adulation he got from the crowd was something I never forgot. I can't honestly remember when I made my first

147, but the buzz I got from doing it never changed throughout my career and I loved having people watch me when I did it.

I never really saw the point in having a table and playing shots that nobody would see. It didn't really thrill me to go for centuries either, but 147s were different. That's why I ended up going for blacks all the time, because I always wanted to reach that magic figure. When Gary and I were practising, once the first red was potted, if I wasn't on the black we'd set the balls up again. That was how bad it got!

I wouldn't say I was obsessed with making a 147 every time I went to the table, but there was certainly an element of wanting to make a maximum break whenever I could. The one time when I didn't try to make a 147 was two or three days before a major tournament. I knew that in order to try and play well and reach the latter stages I would sometimes have to 'play ugly' to win matches and so the focus of my practice changed to accommodate this.

In all, I made 196 maximum breaks during my career, a record figure which earned me the nickname of 'Mr Maximum'. Sadly, only one of those 147s was achieved during a tournament, against Tommy Murphy during the UK Championship at Preston in 1987. That was a proud moment, but it was another maximum break that really stands out for very different reasons.

There were always different things being organised at the club and some of the boys used to love going to Newark to race around on go-karts. On one occasion I decided to go with them. I asked Gary if he wanted to come along as well, but there was no way he was going to join in. By this time Gary was in Leicester City's first team so he didn't want to risk getting an injury. When I told him I was going to have a go he said I was mad, and told me that I could end up breaking my legs. Needless to say, I took no notice of him and duly turned up at the track with the rest of the lads. We were all having a great time bombing around and acting like a bunch of kids and then all of a sudden there was a bang as one of the karts hit the tyres that act as safety buffers on the perimeter of the course, sending both the machine and its driver flying. It was unfortunate for him and, as it turned out, for me too because both man and machine landed on my legs.

The pain was incredible and I knew I was in trouble. I was rushed to hospital and diagnosed with a fractured right leg and a badly damaged left foot. After they had patched me up and plastered both legs, Gary's words came back to haunt me. I hadn't thought it through and just didn't believe there was any real risk involved. Gary, on the other hand, wasn't going to put his career as a professional footballer in jeopardy by courting avoidable injuries. When the local press found out they couldn't resist stunting up a picture of the two of us when he visited me in my hospital bed. The shot showed me sitting there with my legs in plaster and Gary gently sliding a snooker cue between two of my toes.

Of course, just like Gary, I too was a professional sportsman. I had to take time out from playing the game for a while, but there was one particular engagement that I decided to take part in. Every year the Post Office used to organise a snooker competition for its employees, with games staged all around the country. The culmination of this came at my Snooker Centre when we held a dinner and I would play their champion over three frames. On this particular occasion I was still on crutches as I recovered from my karting mishap, but decided I would try to make the most of it, using the edge of the table and the crutches to prop myself up as best I could as I played my shots. To everyone's surprise and delight, including my own, I managed to make a 147 break amid wild applause from the audience.

Although Gary respotted the blacks for a lot of my 147s at the club, we played together so often that he began to develop his own break-building. He went about his business very methodically and was capable of making century breaks. If we played ten frames, he would usually take at least one off me. There was no doubt he loved the game, but in the mid-Eighties when he left the country to play in Spain his regular snooker sessions began to dry up, and I think he then began to concentrate more on his golf, which has always been of a very good standard as well.

It has been great watching Gary's career, first as a footballer and then in more recent years as he has developed into one of the top sports presenters on television. Nothing he has achieved has surprised me because I could see the drive and desire he had way back in those snooker-playing days, and I think we both loved seeing each other doing well in our respective sports all of those years ago.

It's ironic to think that Gary once jokingly said to me that he wished he was a snooker player, because at the time I was making so much money from what I was doing, while he was still making a relatively modest amount as a professional footballer with Leicester. All that was to change for him of course, but I think it was also an indication of just where snooker was in the boom years of the 1980s. The game really began to take off in the early part of the decade, while football at the highest level in this country was nothing like it is now. Footballers in Britain earned decent money, but snooker players were beginning to reap the rewards that television exposure had brought, as the audience for the televised tournaments grew by the million.

The snooker club was a great success for our family and I think we showed the way forward for others at that time, because a lot more clubs began to open up and I don't think the appetite for the game had ever been greater. The success of the club also coincided with more professional success for me. Getting the monkey off my back with that first win in the Pontins Spring Open certainly helped, and it was nice to go out and play games knowing that at last I was a winner. I think anyone involved in such an individual sport as snooker will tell you just how psychologically important getting that first win is. It kind of reaffirms what you have been thinking and telling yourself. That you are a good player and it is only a matter of time before the win comes along. The trouble is, the longer it takes the more the self-doubts begin to creep in and if that happens during the course of a match you are clearly at a disadvantage, because you become twitchy and less able to play your natural game. That's when your opponent can take advantage.

As I have mentioned, one of the things which I believe contributed to me not winning more tournaments than I did was my mental fragility. I don't think I ever fully conquered my fear of losing. I certainly wanted to win any match I played in, but the fear of not doing so was always lurking at the back of my mind, and I never fully got rid of it.

Having won at Pontins, I felt I was maturing as a player, and was more at home in the professional game than I had been when I first started. The following year I reached the final of the Pontins Professional Championship, losing 9-8 to Terry Griffiths, and the year after I had a good run in the World Championship, which by now had become an annual fixture at the Crucible Theatre in Sheffield. The Crucible hadn't exactly been a happy hunting ground for me, but on this particular occasion the tournament came around at the right time. For whatever reason, all the elements of my game were beginning to slot into place. It had taken a while for it to happen, but once it did I felt a lot happier with the way I was playing and at last I began to get some consistency into my game. I played well and managed to reach the quarter-final stage, which was in marked contrast to my previous appearances because I hadn't managed to win a match in the World Championship for six years. That changed in 1982 during a tournament that proved eventful for me both on and off the snooker table.

To reach the quarter-finals, I'd had comfortable wins over former world champions, Terry Griffiths (10-6) and John Spencer (13-5), so, naturally, I was feeling confident. Not only had I broken my losing streak, I'd also managed to beat two of the game's big guns along the way, so I had every reason to feel good about my chances of beating my quarter-final opponent Alex Higgins. He was in fine form too, but because of the way I had sailed through in the previous rounds with my game feeling very solid, I was very confident I could take care of him. I was probably in the best form of my life so there was no reason not to be confident about the outcome.

The Crucible is a venue which provides a tremendous atmosphere, and it was always special to play there, but I have to say that it was never my favourite as a player. The two-table set-up was very cramped and claustrophobic (it is not until the semi-final stage that they revert to one table). You sat close to your opponent, and there was just something about the arena which I was never comfortable with. That doesn't mean it isn't a very special place and as a tournament the World Championship always seems to produce great drama. It has a magical atmosphere like no other, but in practical terms, as a player back then, I could never fully relax into it, even when I was doing well.

About a week or so before I was due in Sheffield I'd experienced a different sort of drama in my personal life, when it looked at one stage as if I might get shot! At the time I was having an affair with a married woman, although as far as I was concerned her marriage was pretty much over, and her husband was someone I knew. He used to come into the club all the time and I was on friendly terms with him, but his brother somehow got wind of what was happening and wasn't too pleased, so he took it upon himself to break the news to the woman's husband. The first time I heard of this was when I got a phone call from the woman in question telling me that her husband had driven off in his car and she knew he had a gun with him. He apparently liked to go hunting and when she saw that the gun was missing from its case she immediately alerted me. I could understand him being upset, and I could also understand that he might want to confront me about what had gone on, but when you throw into the equation the fact that he was carrying a gun as well, the whole scenario took on a much more sinister and frightening aspect. Malcolm immediately went into his older brother protective mode and insisted that he locked me safely in one of the rooms at the club until the police, who by this time had been told of what might be about to happen, caught up with the aggrieved husband.

It was all pretty heavy stuff and the police finally found the guy, but not before they had set up roadblocks and cornered him in true crime drama fashion. He did have his gun with him, but it quickly transpired that he hadn't gone off in a blind rage to try and find me; he simply needed a bit of space and time to think after being told about the affair to try to come to terms with it. The gun was missing because he'd been shooting the day before and, although I'm sure he was upset with what he'd learned about me and his wife, there was no way he was on his way over to the club to try and shoot me. In the end there was no harm done to me, and I was left to concentrate on trying to do well in the World Championship. And despite all that had gone on, the husband continued to be friendly towards me and would later come to some of the tournaments I played in. He and his wife did try to make another go of it, but the marriage didn't last.

It was all very unfortunate and we all do things in our private lives that perhaps we're not that proud of, and I certainly wasn't the first and won't be the last man to have an affair with a married woman. The difference is that for most people such an episode in their lives would remain private between the individuals involved, but when you enter a high-profile profession that whole situation changes. You could say I was stupid to have the affair in the first place and that might be true, but on top of that I was also naive. I stupidly underestimated the power of the press in this country and the appetite of the general public for a good old-fashioned tabloid story. As a consequence, on the eve of the biggest match in my professional snooker career up to that point, when my sole focus should have been on playing Alex Higgins, the whole story was splashed across a red-top newspaper for the world to read – or at least for everyone who was going to be in the Crucible watching me try to beat Higgins.

It was a horrible feeling when I walked out to the table to face Alex, because I felt all eyes were on me. I couldn't hide from what had been written and, as is often the case, the timing of it gave the story its maximum impact. Beating Alex Higgins at the best of times was always difficult, but I certainly didn't need all the publicity concerning my private life to contend with as well.

I knew I had to try and put it all to one side and just get on with the match, which wasn't exactly easy, but at least I was in the form of my life and that gave me a lot of encouragement. Once I started playing, I felt better; it was thinking about the story in the paper and what people thought of me that I found the hardest thing to have to cope with.

Alex was his usual erratic self and he made a nasty comment about me being willing to stab my own grand-mother for 50p. I thought it was a very disrespectful thing to say, but I'm afraid Alex was always capable of doing something like that. You just didn't know what you were going to get from him, and our relationship during the match wasn't exactly the friendliest. There were a few comments exchanged and the atmosphere, quite literally, wasn't helped by the fact that Alex had about ten cigarettes on the go at the same time, smouldering away in an ashtray.

Having gone into the match feeling distinctly uneasy because of the tabloid story, I actually began to play well and showed the sort of form I had displayed in previous rounds. In one frame, I potted the first six reds with blacks, and was feeling so confident that I called up to my mum who was in the audience: "Do we need a maximum, Mum?"

Malcolm had driven me up from Leicester that morning and he was sitting next to her. Before my mother could reply, he chirped up with the sort of common-sense advice I needed.

"No," he said. "Just win the frame!"

I did exactly that and managed to do it with a 143 break, which proved to be the highest of the tournament that year. We finished the first session even, but I eventually ended up losing the match 13-10 and being eliminated from a tournament which Alex went on to win.

I still think that year was my best-ever chance of winning the World Championship. My game was really good at the time, I'd proved in the match against John Spencer that I was one of the best players around and it was a real chance for me to go all the way. It was such a shame that it ended as it did. Ultimately my defeat wasn't down to the fact that the newspaper article had been published, it was about me not being able to get the better of Alex.

He was a great player, who could be ruthless at the table. There's no doubt he was a one-off character who had the ability to be charming one moment and quite nasty on other occasions. He could spit out comments like the one I have described and not think about the consequences of his actions and how hurtful they might be.

To be fair to Alex, he was always pretty good whenever he stayed at our place and was nice to my mum, but over the years I had plenty of moments where he really got under my skin and upset me. When that happened he would be on the phone two days later saying sorry. Alex was a loner in so many ways, but at the same time he liked having company and he always needed mothering, whether it was by my own mum or other players who he was friendly with.

I remember on a trip to Canada once I bought a teddy bear from him as a present for a girlfriend I had at the time back in England. I'd left it late to get her anything and so in desperation I agreed a price with Alex for the bear, which he had won at a fairground close to the venue for an exhibition a few of us had been playing. Everyone seemed to be able to win one of these bears except me.

On the plane back to England the next day Alex had a few too many drinks and became drunk quite quickly. He then tried to grab the bear off me, and the two of us ended up having a bit of a fight, with me giving him a slap before the rest of the lads separated us.

Alex was capable of upsetting anyone and there is no doubt at all that he was a genuine eccentric. On another occasion we were staying in the same hotel and I was fast asleep when I got a call from him. He was staying about two rooms down the corridor and wanted me to go and see him.

"Alex have you any idea what the time is?" I asked him.

"I know, I know, Willie, but there's something I want you to see," he told me.

So, half asleep, I trooped out of my room and walked the short distance along the corridor before knocking on the door. Alex opened it displaying his manhood to show me that he had just shaved off all of his pubic hair.

"What do you think?" he asked.

"Very nice Alex," I told him as I stifled a yawn, turned on my heels and walked back to my room.

It wasn't worth trying to ask him why he'd done such a crazy sort of thing, it was just another mad moment from Alex, and throughout the time I knew him there were plenty of them. On the whole, Alex tended to be fine until he'd had that one drink too many and then it would tip him over the edge and he could become a different character. Every time I played him in an exhibition we'd have a little side bet for maybe £200 and then in the hotel I'd have a game of cards with him, which was great for me because he was a hopeless card player.

You never quite knew what you were getting with Alex, but I did like him and he was always a welcome visitor whenever he wanted to come and stay in Leicester. He often used my Snooker Centre as a practice base if he was playing a tournament in or around the area, with my mother more than happy to look after him and make sure his shirts and suit were ironed and pressed. That was probably why I found his comments during that quarter-final so hurtful.

Mum continued to be a big supporter of mine, and knowing she was there in the background definitely helped me. I was still living at home at that time, although I really only used it as a base because I was out so much. She was always trying to give me good advice and boost my confidence. She would iron all of my shirts for tournaments and quite often she would slip in little notes of encouragement for me to read. Nothing elaborate, just short phrases which she hoped would help, things like 'I can' or 'I will'. She was also very keen that I should behave in a certain way when I played my snooker, and I remember her saying to me once, "I don't care if you lose, so long as you always come off the table like a gentleman." I may have done some things in my life which I am not proud of, but I think I always made sure I didn't let her down in that respect.

CHAPTER SEVEN

ON TOP OF
THE WORLD

Losing to Alex Higgins in the quarter-finals of the World Championship was a blow because it had been such a great opportunity for me, but at least I had the satisfaction of knowing that I played really well in the tournament and had notched up the highest break. It was certainly something I could build on for the future, and it was also clear that I could compete with and beat the best players in the game. Appearing on television meant I was becoming better known, too. I suppose I had quite a distinctive look with my balding head and big black moustache and at six feet two inches I'm quite tall so I tended to stand out in a crowd.

I started to lose my hair when I was about 21, and at the time I wasn't too pleased about it as you can imagine. It made me look quite a bit older than I was, and when you're that age things like that matter a lot. But when I did start to look at the alternatives I quickly came to the conclusion that it was better to swallow my pride rather than wear some of the wigs I looked at, and the thought of a hair transplant didn't exactly thrill me either. Once I'd got over the initial worries about my appearance it got a lot easier for me and in the end I came to terms with what was happening and let nature take its course. I think the alternative would have been to look ridiculous and that would have been even worse. In later years I was grateful for it, simply because my appearance left an impression and made me one of the most recognisable faces on the snooker circuit, which was good for my career.

I'm happy to say that my lack of hair never seemed to hold me back with the ladies. I might not have been the best-looking bloke in the world, but I was always a good talker and found it easy to chat to women and get along with them. In 1980, I began to see a young girl called Fiona, who I'd met at a local nightclub and bar where she worked. I started chatting to her and we got on really well, but because of my thinning hair she actually thought I was about 15 years older than I was. She was even a bit concerned about her parents meeting me because of that, believing they would think she was going out with a much older man, but I soon put her straight about exactly how old I was and there was actually no more than four years between us. We began to see quite a bit of each other and started a relationship that would eventually see us marry and have three children.

Having been a regular at the racecourses around Britain for some years, a lot of people in the business knew me and what I did for a living, but once my face became better known to the general public in the early Eighties I gave up the very enjoyable business of tick-tacking for Raymond. I still went to the courses, though, and my enthusiasm for racing and for having a bet on the horses never waned. In fact, I was more enthusiastic about it than ever. I also had more money than I had ever had. Gambling was just as much a way of life as it had been ever since I had my first serious bet, and I still had the same group of friends from my days at Osborne's. It was always nice turning up to play knowing so many of my mates were in the audience giving me their support. My only regret was that I hadn't really given them too much to cheer in terms of winning competitions. There were certainly some highs when I played really well and won matches, but as in any other sport, the ultimate measure of success is winning tournaments.

In between winning that Pontins Spring Open in 1980 and losing to Higgins in the World Championship in 1982, I reached another final, of the 1981 Pontins Professional tournament, but ended up losing 9-8 to Terry Griffiths. It was a disappointment, but at the same time it showed that I was one of the up-and-coming players on the circuit, and my performance at Sheffield the following year backed that up.

I knew I was making progress, even if the rate was frustratingly slow at times. In 1983, I reached my first semi-final in a ranking tournament in the Grand Prix but failed to go one step further and make it to the final. Happily, the disappointment of that year was forgotten about in 1984 with an important win that boosted my confidence and status in the game. Once again it was the Pontins Professional tournament, but this time I managed to take the trophy, beating John Spencer 9-7 in the final. It was great to get another tournament win under my belt, even if it had been a four-year wait since I last tasted victory. But I think it was more than just a win. I believe it was the start of me hitting the sort of form that made me one of the best players around in the mid-Eighties, just when the game's popularity was reaching its peak in the UK.

Snooker became a firm favourite with the public who loved watching tournaments on television, and the viewing figures went through the roof. The top players were recognised everywhere they went and, along with the fame and popularity, the game also experienced a big increase in the sort of money that was on offer. Gone were the days of the early and mid-Seventies when it was really more profitable for me to stay as an amateur and earn money from playing matches in billiard halls. *Pot Black* had started something that not even the television executives could have believed would become so popular. The game fitted perfectly onto a TV screen, you could see the table and all of the balls at the same time, the close-ups allowed the viewers to experience some of the tension players were feeling and the whole format of competitive professional snooker was something which really caught the imagination of the public. I've had people come up to me and say that they weren't even really interested in snooker, but started watching it and then couldn't stop.

I can't really tell you what the appeal of the game was and why it became so popular at that time. I think people appreciated the skill involved and also took to the players who were competing. There's no doubt it was a golden era for the game, and although snooker is still very popular and the figures for the really big tournaments are still very healthy I don't think the 1980s will ever be matched in this country. It went from being a game played in in working men's clubs and billiard halls, to mainstream television. I think all of the players who were around at that time helped to set it on a different course. Today's players have continued to reap the rewards from what we did back then. Without overstating it, we were pioneers, simply because we were doing things which hadn't been done before, popularising the game on television and then taking it to other countries around the world.

My form at that time was good enough to get me into the top 16 players and in the 1983/84 season I was ranked seventh in the world. I also reached the final of the World Snooker Doubles tournament in 1984, playing alongside my good friend, Cliff Thorburn. Cliff was a real character and had really made a name for himself by becoming world champion in 1980. He was one of a handful of Canadians who made a big impact on the snooker circuit, along with the likes of big Bill Werbeniuk and Kirk Stevens.

Cliff was one of the funniest people I've ever met, and we have remained friends for a long time. During the Eighties, we decided to go on holiday to St. Lucia together with our young families for a relaxing break, but within days we began to wonder if we'd made a huge mistake.

It is no secret that during the course of his career Cliff used marijuana, and on the first day of our holiday Cliff headed into town to try and purchase some of the stuff.

He turned up back at the hotel with a package he bought from one of the locals only to discover when he unwrapped it he'd been sold regular tobacco. Cliff had been duped.

A day later one of my twin boys, Kieran, who had just about started to walk, managed to lock himself in the bathroom and we had to get some hotel maintenance men to take the door off as our son screamed the place down. Soon after that Kieran's twin, Tristan, managed to run into a set of patio doors thinking they were open, and then the next day Kieran picked something up off the beach and ate, it leading to him having a raging temperature which only subsided when he was placed in a bath full of ice.

We'd only been there a couple of days and it was turning into the holiday from hell, but there was still more to come. A day later, Cliff and I were swimming in the sea with his wife Barbara when a huge wave hit her from behind. I hadn't been aware that she had a few false teeth at the top of her mouth, but I soon realised something was wrong when Barbara emerged from the water minus her front teeth! They'd been knocked out by the force of the wave, and in the end Cliff and I had to call on the help of half a dozen local guys to go diving under the water in an effort to find the dentures. We never did manage to, and poor Barbara spent about 48 hours wandering around the place covering up her mouth before a local dentist provided her with a replacement set of dentures. Thankfully, things calmed down a bit after that, but none of us could believe how so many things could have gone wrong in such a short period of time.

As a part of those boom years for snooker, the appeal of

the game began to spread to all sorts of places around the globe, including Canada, and I was one of the first British snooker players to be invited to play on the circuit out there.

The game was still playing second fiddle to pool, but there were some very decent snooker players apart from the three I have already mentioned – names like Brady Gollan, Jim Wych and Bob Chaperon. My first trip to Canada was with John Virgo, who I'd known since our junior days. He'd come up through the ranks in very much the same way I had, and his billiard hall background meant that we had a lot in common. We got on really well, had some great times together while we were out there and as a result became good friends. Together, we tried to raise the profile of the sport in Canada and get it more commonly accepted, which was always going to be a battle against pool.

That first trip to Canada led to another and then another – in all I competed for 10 seasons in Canada and always enjoyed my time there. Like all of the Canadians, Cliff realised that if he was ever going to fulfil his potential as a professional snooker player he needed to come to Britain, and my connection with Canada also meant that a lot of the boys who played over there got to know me well. When Cliff decided to come over to England he would quite often stay with us, with my mum once again fussing over him, as she did for whichever players I turned up with. In fact, Cliff's fellow Canadian, Bill Werbeniuk, once turned up at my mum's and stayed for about six months! We became very good friends and Bill, like a lot of other players, used to like making his base in Leicester when I had the snooker club, because it gave him a place to practise regularly and he could travel to the various tournaments around the country. Unfortunately, my relationship with Bill soured some years later when he sold a story to a Sunday newspaper claiming that I owed him money and also dished some dirt on other players on the professional circuit. In fact, it was Bill who owed me money, and as soon as the story was published he headed back to Canada. I never spoke to him again after that and wasn't ever able to put things right with him before he died in 2003 at the age of just 56.

With my own game in a lot better shape by the mid-Eighties, I knew that I could be a serious challenger for some of the big ranking titles. I knew I had it within me when it came to my ability, but I was also very much aware that I was going to have to display more mental toughness if I was going to get the sort of win I wanted. I was recognised as one of the best players in the game at the time, but I still needed that special win. Having reached the semi-final of the Grand Prix, I was determined to improve on that performance and go one better by getting to a final and winning one of the game's big ranking tournaments. I had been close on too many occasions and I also knew that I was getting a reputation as someone who could play, but also someone who might not be able to pull off one of the big ones. I wanted to be known as a player who could perform at the highest level and that meant winning a ranking tournament.

My chance came in the Mercantile Credit Classic played

in Warrington in 1985, but I went into the tournament feeling that I wasn't going to be hanging around for too long. In fact, I was so convinced that this would be another big one that would pass me by, that I didn't even bother packing more than a couple of shirts. The reason for this was that my form in the week or two before the tournament started had really taken a dip. In practice I just didn't seem to be able to hit the shots I wanted and I was sure I was going to have to wait a bit longer for success.

In the past I would often go into a tournament feeling really good because I thought my form was just right, only to be proved wrong when I started to play. As it turned out, the complete opposite was true this time. I had thought I would be out and on my way back to Leicester after a couple of rounds, but for once everything seemed to click and my snooker really began to flow as I knew it could. Everything just seemed right, which was a very pleasant surprise to me.

I had to start sending home for extra shirts as I fought my way through to the final and the chance to finally win a ranking tournament. I had great preparation because in the semi-final I had to overcome Steve Davis, and any victory over him was not only well earned, it also served as a great confidence boost simply because you knew just how good and consistent Steve was.

The man who stood in my way in the final was none other than Cliff Thorburn. He knew how much I wanted to win and we knew a lot about each other's games. Having seen Cliff at close quarters back in Canada as well as in this country, I knew it wasn't going to be easy, but I was very confident in my own ability to finally get a really big victory to my name. As usual, I had great support in the crowd from my family and friends, including another local Leicester boy, boxer Tony Sibson, as well as Gary Lineker and some of his footballing pals, like Phil Neal and Bruce Grobbelaar, as well as my gambling crowd from Osborne's. It's always nice to know you have support when you play big matches and I wanted to make sure I gave them a win to celebrate. I didn't feel any added pressure, but at the same time I knew it was a great opportunity for me to pull off the win I wanted. The prize money for winning it was £40,000, which was a huge amount at the time, but I'd also had a bet on myself to go all the way and knew that if I won, I would pick up a further £10,000. Despite not feeling optimistic, I'd still placed bets on myself through the various contacts I had in the gambling world, and they in turn had probably had a few bob on me as well. I can't remember the sort of odds I got, but I think some of the pricing would have been influenced by the fact that Cliff was the favourite, although I knew I had a great record against him just as I did against Dennis Taylor, so the fact that they might have been perceived as better players didn't really come into it. I knew I could win.

My mental attitude that day was just what it needed to be. All matches ebb and flow, and there are good and bad phases of play for each player; the important thing is to maintain your nerve and keep your concentration, no matter what happens. Cliff had a reputation for being able to wear people out and plough his way to victory. He had the nickname of the 'Grinder' because he could do just that – grind out wins. But on this occasion, with around 12 million people tuning in to see the final on television, I felt in control of the situation and pretty much everything seemed to go well for me. In the end, I won the final 13-8 and always felt I was going to get across the finishing line with a bit to spare.

All the self-doubts and mental frailty I had so often displayed at other crucial moments in my snooker career were absent as I finally managed to get the my first ranking win. It was nice for all the people who had supported me and given me encouragement. My mum and dad certainly enjoyed the moment, as did my brothers. My gambling pals backed me as usual and were not only happy because I'd won, but also because, like me, they'd got some money for themselves.

The strange thing was that after all the effort and emotion which went into winning the game I was left feeling a bit empty. It was all something of an anti-climax. I had waited a long time to actually win a ranking tournament, but if I'm honest the feeling I got from it was no different to when I'd won at Pontins. It was nice to win, but there was no difference for me. I think it mattered more to other people than it did to myself. My mother was particularly pleased and it was lovely to see the pleasure in her eyes as she posed for pictures with me and the trophy. I was now the winner of a ranking tournament, but there was no great feeling of elation for me, other than the initial relief when I'd finally got myself past the winning post and captured the title.

I'd spent a long time trying to get a big win and, no matter what else I'd done as a professional player, I realised that a lot of people were only going to judge me on winning major events. I suppose that in many ways it's like a golfer or tennis player who is clearly talented and maybe wins lots of events each year, but never gets his hands on a major or a grand slam title. That kind of career fact can haunt people, and it's even more frustrating if you know that you have the talent and ability to win but fall short for one reason or another.

Just like that first-ever win at Pontins, there was a sense that some of the pressure had lifted off me but, despite going on to have a great deal of success and enjoying a good career as a snooker player, that victory in 1985 remained my one and only ranking tournament success. Even now, that fact has me shaking my head in disbelief because, without wishing to sound arrogant, I know I should have won a lot more than that. There were, of course, other victories in other tournaments, but ranking event wins are what a lot of people will measure you by and, had my mental state matched my natural ability, I believe I would have ended up with more than just that lone triumph. I didn't do myself justice, and to this day I still regret it.

After that win in the Mercantile, my life looked pretty good. I had won a top tournament, I had money, fame and the future looked bright. Snooker's popularity continued to grow, and 1985 proved to be a big year for me in more ways than one. Not only did I have that win, but I also married Fiona after we had lived together for the previous four years in a flat close to my snooker club. We were happy enough together without getting married, but then Fiona became pregnant and we decided to tie the knot in what turned out to be quite a lavish affair. By this time I was something of a local celebrity, and it seemed like pretty much everyone in Leicester knew we were going to get married, with crowds coming out to watch us in the village of Oadby, where the wedding was held. It was a lovely day, with all my snooker mates there as well as quite a few people from the world of entertainment, including TV sports presenter Dickie Davies and Leicester City footballer Alan Smith. Gary Lineker acted as my best man, and the reception was held near to the church where we were married. It all went really well.

Like any wedding, the cost soon mounted up. Fortunately, I was earning quite a lot in those days and I was lucky enough not to have to worry about where the money was going to come from. It was a good job I didn't because the manager of the place where we had the reception did a runner with the £2,000 deposit I had given him for the food! Like me, he was a gambler, and he just vanished two days after I had given him the cash. I suspect he must have got into financial trouble with his gambling and saw my money as a quick way out. If my experience in later years was anything to go by, it would have only acted as a temporary solution, and I have to say that, although I did some desperate things when I was in need of some cash, I never actually resorted to nicking money.

In August, Fiona gave birth to twin boys, Tristan and Kieran. I was now a married man with a family to support but, although I am not proud of the fact, I was not the most faithful of husbands. Once again, I have to own up to having the sort of weakness in my character that allowed me to succumb to temptation on many occasions when it came to women.

Like any other red-blooded man, being attracted to women was just a natural part of my life. Where things probably differed for me was that, because of my fame and the type of job I did, the opportunity to stray was always present. People can point a finger at me and say that, although there was the opportunity, it didn't mean I had to take it, and I agree. My only defence is that I was too weak and that the chance to go off with other women was all too easy, especially when snooker took me away from home so often and also for long periods at a time, and that was really when I began to stray; I certainly never met women close to home.

It may sound strange, but I actually never really saw it as being unfaithful or having affairs. In my own mind, I put the episodes in their own little compartment. I still loved Fiona and my family. I didn't see it as something that was harming them, because the two parts of my life were separate. One never needed to interfere or impinge on the other. I know it is ridiculous and a warped way of looking at things, but I suppose that was how I was able to live with what I was doing without feeling bad about myself. I'm sure many men justify being unfaithful to their wives and partners to themselves in the same way.

It is not something I am proud of now, but it happened. Fiona actually found out about a couple of affairs I had, but she was willing to forgive me and we carried on together. We had a couple of young boys whom we both loved dearly and our lifestyle was fantastic at that time. With the sort of earning capacity I had at that midpoint in the 1980s, I should have been guaranteed a lifetime of happiness and prosperity.

If I had only stuck to snooker I'm sure that would have been the case, but there was something else lurking in the background that had become an increasingly important part of my life and which was to eventually overwhelm me. I didn't know it at the time, but the gambling bug that I had been bitten by all of those years ago was slowly and surely beginning to take more of a hold. At the time I thought nothing of it, but looking back now the warning signs were all there, I just chose to ignore them, and that has been a common theme with me throughout my life. There have been moments where if I had stood back and given a bit of thought to what I was doing and where it might all be leading, so much might have been different. Lots of other people would have done just that, and the outcome would not have been the same for them, but that wasn't me. I always enjoyed life, and my snooker exploits allowed me to live it to the full. Sure, I was gambling heavily, but I was having a good time doing it and, in my own mind, I was always going to be able to fund my betting, because I was earning some very serious money from snooker.

Winning the Mercantile made me a more attractive prop-osition as a player. I was now one of the best in the world, and at one stage I would honestly say that I was probably the second-best player around, with only Steve Davis in front of me. Davis was at the heart of what his manager Barry Hearn was trying to achieve in snooker with his Matchroom stable of players, and it wasn't too long before I was invited to join them and be part of something which

I now genuinely believe revolutionised the game. There was no doubt that snooker was popular, but Barry used his innate skills as a businessman and promoter to take the game to another level. He could see just how popular it had become in this country, and he made sure that the market in Britain continued to grow, but perhaps his biggest achievement was the way in which he moved into hitherto untapped markets. Barry opened up new opportunities for us at the time and in doing so left a legacy which is still evident now. Without what happened back in the 1980s, there simply wouldn't be the number of tournaments around the world that there are today.

It was really as a direct result of winning the Mercantile that Barry asked whether I would be interested in joining Matchroom. To be honest, it didn't take that much thinking about. Barry clearly had some great ideas about how he would market and expand the game. He wanted a group of top players who could help him do that, and I was happy to become part of his plans. The fact that he would take his 20 per cent of everything didn't bother me. I realised that without Barry's ideas, drive and enthusiasm, none of us would have been involved in the sort of things he set up, and let's face it, having 80 per cent of something is far better than having 100 per cent of nothing.

In all, I was with Barry for about seven years, and I can't criticise him. I earned good money because of what he did for all of us, and you couldn't help but admire the way he went about the job of creating a whole new atmosphere and market for snooker to be played in. Barry was always buzzing with ideas, and the way he managed his stable of players was very professional. I think all of us, the players and Barry, benefitted from some of the greatest times the game in this country has seen.

Barry already had Steve Davis, Dennis Taylor, Terry Griffiths and Tony Meo at Matchroom, before I came along. I joined and we became the famous five. A little later the likes of Neal Foulds and Jimmy White were also involved in Matchroom projects. We even had our own tournament, which I won in 1987, the first year in which it was played. In typical Barry fashion, he managed to attract good sponsorship, television coverage and media attention for that first championship, which was contested exclusively by the Matchroom players. In the final I came up against Steve Davis and, as always, knew I was going to have my work cut out if I was going to beat him, but I did it and won, making a break of 80 in the final frame. I suppose that victory went some way to helping make up for a double whammy of defeats Davis had inflicted on me, beating me in the final of two very big tournaments, the British Open in 1986 and the UK Championship a year earlier.

In the Open at the Brighton Centre, I lost out 12-7. To the outside observer, 1986 looked a pretty good year for me in terms of the way I was playing and what I achieved in some of the big tournaments. Once again, I got to the quarter-final stage in the World Championship, I also won the Hong Kong Masters, but although I got to the final of the Pontins Professional tournament, as I had two years earlier, I went down 9-6 to Terry Griffiths. However, it was the defeat to Davis in the ranking tournament which put a real dampener on the year.

My loss to him in 1985 in the UK Championships at Preston was even worse. Painful. I had played well to reach the final and fancied myself to go all the way. It was a 31-frame match, and I got myself into a strong position by taking a 13-8 lead, just three frames away from victory. As a top player with that sort of lead, you really should be able to close the game out and go on to win the match. Your opponent should be the one worrying about trying to make up such a margin, knowing you only need a few frames to secure the victory. There's an awful lot of pressure on the player trailing in the game and it's that as much as anything else which can prove a decisive factor. Not only do they have to play well, they also have to do so in the knowledge they're running out of frames in which to pull things around. So on the face of it, everything was set up for me to go on and win the match, beating the player who was rated the best in the world at that time, but that wasn't taking into account what was now a definite Achilles heel in my own game, namely the fragile state of my mind when I got myself into just such situations. There is no doubt that I could and should have won that day in Preston, but after getting myself into such a strong position it all began to unravel for me, first in my head and then as a consequence of that, on the snooker table.

Before going into that final session, I had a visit in my hotel from an old friend when Gary Lineker popped in to try and give me a confidence boost and help make sure I made it over the line. Gary quite rightly pointed out that if I went out in the final session and won the first frame, Steve would then need eight frames to overhaul me, but it was the psychological impact would be enormous. That would put Steve six behind, and he would only be able to afford to lose one more frame. Effectively, the match would pretty much be over. I told Gary he was absolutely right and also said that I thought there was no way Davis could get back into the game, because I was playing some really good snooker just when I needed to. I went out for that final session feeling good about myself and with the sort of confidence I knew I needed in order to see the job through, but somehow the thought of what Gary had said kept playing in my mind. 'Win the first frame, that's all I need,'

I didn't start the frame very well and soon found myself trailing by 40 points, but began to claw my way back, reaffirming the way I felt about my own game. It was in good shape, and it seemed as though this really was going to be my day. After I had potted the final four reds on the table I moved onto the colours. The first three went in without too much trouble, setting me up for the blue. By this time I was feeling very confident because it all seemed to be going my way. I stunned the cue ball so that I would have the perfect position to pot the pink with my next shot, but instead of seeing the blue roll into the pocket as I was sure it would when I hit my shot, the thing jawed instead, staying out and leaving me staring in disbelief at what had just happened. It all happened in seconds, and as I went back to my seat all the confidence and self-belief seemed to drain from me. I was in shock and all I could hear in my head were Gary's words. He had been right, of course, but instead of finding myself in the position I had wanted, I was now 13-9 ahead instead of the 14-8 I'd hoped for. I started thinking about losing rather than winning as all my past slip-ups on other occasions began to surface in my mind. The positive thoughts were replaced by a host of negative ones as, mentally, I handed the initiative to Davis.

There was no better player in the world for sniffing out a weakness in an opponent. He smelt blood and went for it as I began to crumble. I simply couldn't get my head together after missing that blue and once again my mental frailty proved to be my undoing as Steve went on to win the match 16-14. It was a real blow and I should never have allowed it to happen.

It showed that ability alone means nothing in professional sport. It can only get you so far, but if it's not allied to the sort of mental toughness Steve showed that day then you are always liable to under-achieve. That weakness was the reason for me only ever winning one ranking tournament, and the toughness he displayed was the reason for Davis being as successful as he was.

I was deeply disappointed with the outcome, not only because I had victory within my grasp, but also because I'd backed myself before the tournament and got some very good odds. If I had made it all the way and won the competition I would have stood to have collected around £100,000 from the bookies on top of the prize money I would have got from winning the championship which was around £50,000.

I had slaughtered Steve until it came to that blue ball, that blue ball of extreme simplicity, and it was amazing that he'd stuck in there and managed to win eight frames up until that point, but that's how good he was.

Defeat in that match was a big turning point for me. Even though I went on to have other successes, I began to doubt myself. Deep down I knew that all the excuses I might have made to myself in the past didn't really wash anymore. My bottle had gone against Davis; there was no way of dressing it up, not even to myself, and no matter what sort of front I put on in the future, deep down I knew what had happened and I think a key part of my original game – an unshakeable confidence in my ability – went. That doesn't mean to say I couldn't play to a high standard, because I could; it simply meant that I couldn't kid myself anymore and as such I probably always felt that I was capable of chucking a match away.

I under-achieved and know I should have won more. Having said that, I still believe that my biggest failure was not winning the World Championship when I could have done back in 1982. After all, Dennis Taylor only won one more ranking tournament than me and yet the perception is probably that he had a far more successful career. In fact, Dennis had a great period in 1984 and 1985 – in '84 he won his first ranking tournament with victory in the Rothmans Grand Prix, and then in 1985 he won his second ranking event which just happened to be the world title! Of course, it was a great achievement and the way in which he beat Steve Davis 18-17 on the final black in the final to claim the title rightly went down as one of the most thrilling moments in sporting history.

It was a marvellous win for Dennis, who has been one of my best friends in the game, and having the prestige of being a world champion obviously sets you apart. Dennis

One of the first pictures of me, looking very innocent as a schoolboy.

And here with my dad during one of our holidays in Cromer.

An early experience with the gee gees – I'm at the front with my brother Malcolm.

Celebrating another CIU championship triumph – that's Brian Cakebread holding the trophy.

An early shot of me as a young amateur... pre-moustache and look at all that hair!

My dad dishes out the champagne at his pub after I won the junior championships.

It was tricky to make big breaks with all that silverware on the table!

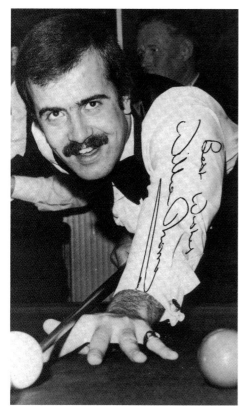

This picture of my mum serving me breakfast appeared in the *Radio Times* after they did a feature on me to publicise *Pot Black*.

My first publcity photo (above) and the business cards I had made when I turned pro (right).

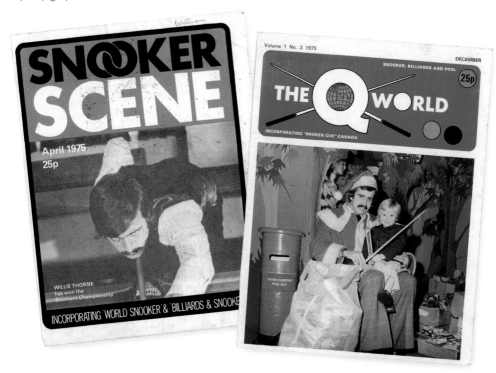

Looking mean and moody – this shot was used for the front cover of the *Radio Times*.

Where it all began. Outside the entrance to Osbornes with my precious snooker cue.

Cliff Thorburn and I play a few trick shots on a special company day at the club.

Serving at 'Willie's Bar' in the club.

Another celebration, another snooker table cake! (From left to right) Racing Raymond, my grandad, me, Mum and a friend of mine, Terry Kirk.

Playing in the World Championships at the Crucible.

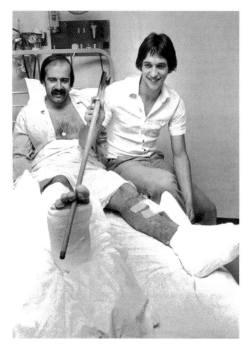

"I told you to not to do it!" Gary Lineker popped in to see me in hospital as I nursed my injuries after my karting accident.

A proud, proud moment. as I finally get my hands on a major trophy – the 1985 Mercantile Credit Classic.

Celebrating with my pals after the Classic. (From the left) Relentless Reg, Billy the Dip, Racing Raymond, me, Captain John, Gary Lineker, boxer Tony Sibson and a friend of his.

Thorne holds 'bottle' party

by Jon Culley

Willie Thorne celebrated into the small hours this morning, still needing to pinch himself periodically after reaching his first major snooker final with a sensational victory over Steve Davis last night.

"I had to keep asking people if I'd really won or if it was just a dream," said Thorne, who goes into the weekend's final of the Mercantile Credit Classic in Warrington, having already achieved the biggest win of his career.

It was the first time Thorne had beaten Davis in a televised event, and his thrilling 9-8 win will probably earn Thorne more prize money than he has won all season regardless of the outcome of the final, to be played over three sessions tomorrow and Sunday.

He triumphed last night in an atmosphere as highly charged as any he has encountered in nine years as a professional, and it was no wonder that the drama of his last-frame victory overcame him in a flood of emotion at the end.

As world champion Davis conceded defeat, Thorne raised his arms above his head to give a double-fisted salute to his Leicester supporters at the Spectrum Arena, and their response quickly brought tears welling in his eyes.

And, outside his dressing room minutes later, as the significance of his seven-hour marathon win began to sink in, Thorne emerged choked and moist-eyed to cheers and embraces from his followers, who included his great friend, Leicester City striker Gary Lineker.

WILLIE THORNE . . . "I just broke up."

"When I saw Gary and all the others, I just broke up," said Thorne.

"My bottle went — but afterwards," he joked, referring to the common claim among his critics that his nerve always fails him on the big occasion.

Thorne has never won a major championship, even though he has never lost a reputation as a skilful player and a prolific break-builder.

In the most dramatic match of the championship, he trailed Davis and recovered four times before taking the lead in the 15th frame, but even then the heart-stopping tension did not end.

and Thorne believed the match was slipping from his grasp in the last when a missed red seemed to have given the millionaire from Romford the chance to make a winning clearance.

"When that happened, I thought 'Oh, no, this is the story of my life'," Thorne said. "But then Steve missed a green that I was amazed he had tried to pot."

Thorne felt he had played his best snooker since he beat Terry Griffiths 10-6 in the first round of the 1982 world championship.

"I played better then, I thought, but obviously this win is more important," he said.

"It is a terrific bonus to be in the final, because after the first two rounds I thought I was lucky still to be in the competition.

Thorne, who was staying in Warrington today to practice and to await the outcome of Cliff Thorburn's semi-final with unseeded Joe Johnson, is bidding for a £40,000 top prize in the final.

But the £24,000 runners-up prize would still represent his biggest tournament earnings, eclipsing the £9,375 he won for finishing second, with Thorburn, in the world doubles championship at Northampton last month.

It may be boosted by £4,000 if the break of 120 in yesterday's match remains the biggest of the tournament.

The newspaper story reporting on my semi-final victory over the great Steve Davis. My mum kept all my cuttings and still has them to this day.

Continuing the celebrations with Mum and Dad.

With my lovely twin boys. That's Kieran with me and Tristan next to my first wife Fiona.

Having fun at home with the boys...

... and living life to the full in snooker's heyday.

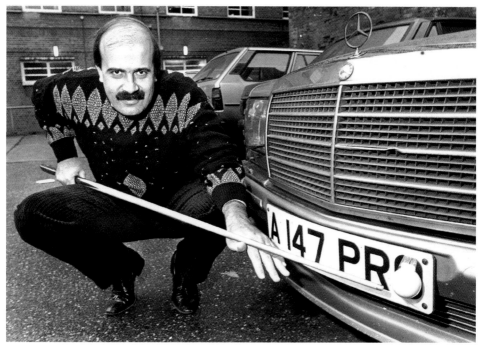

It was the perfect numberplate for 'Mr Maximum'.

Some terrible publicity cards I had made – seemed like a good idea at the time!

Willie is so blue . . .

Leicester snooker star Willie Thorne wears a rueful smile as he reflects on the missed blue which may have cost him the championship. Full story and other pictures on Pages 25 and 28.

Betting on Willie!

Leicester snooker ace Willie Thorne's devoted fans have a special reason to hope he wins this weekend's Coral UK Championship Final against Steve Davis.

If Thorne beats the former world champion at Preston, his supporters will land £250,000 in bets.

Full story on Back Page.

The press made a big thing about how much money my friends had made by betting on me to win the 1985 Coral UK Championships. But it all went wrong in the final...

Barry Hearn with the Matchroom crew in the golden era of snooker when the big tournaments were watched by millions and we earned more than First Divison footballers.

I often partnered my old chum Cliff Thorburn in doubles matches. An easy game against Alex Higgins and Jimmy White this one!

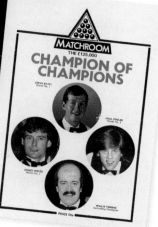

Snooker Loopy. Me with Tony Meo, Terry Griffiths, Dave Peacock, Chas Hodges, Dennis Taylor and Steve Davis – don't ask what we were doing because I have absolutely no idea!

Model Linda Lusardi and I opened about 15 First Frame snooker clubs together.

When I went on a tour of New Zealand they gave me my own personalised car to drive around the country in.

When Gary Lineker signed for Barcelona in 1986 I went over there to spend a week with him and we had a lot of fun. As you can see I hadn't learned my lesson from the go-karting accident!

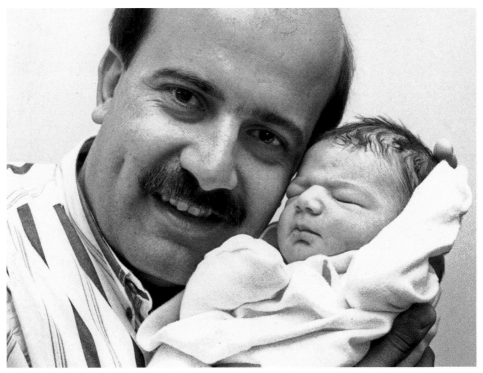

Cuddling my new-born baby daughter Tahli.

Happy Birthday Mum... I think this was for a Mother's Day feature in the *Leicester Mercury*.

Tristan showing his ability with the cue, while Kieran and Dad (background) look on.

We had so much fun and it was as if we'd known each other all our lives.

Jill was Miss Great Britain in 1985, but it wasn't just her looks I fell in love with.

This was our first family holiday all together, Jill and I and all our children, in Tenby in 1994. (From left to right) Kieran, James, Jill, me, Tahli, Natalie and Tristan.

Willie Thorne
Testimonial
Year 2002

LAUNCH PARTY
DINNER DANCE
&
CABARET
THURSDAY 31ST JANUARY

Lumbers

Lumbers Jewellers are supporting tonight's event

My testimonial year was a great success and I had wonderful support from other former sports stars including (left to right) Tommy Docherty, Gary Lineker and Devon Malcolm.

I love hosting sports dinners and auctions, they give me the buzz that I miss now that I've hung up my cue.

Although I was only on the show for a few weeks, I absolutely loved my time on *Strictly Come Dancing* and my partner, Erin Boag, was a wonderful teacher – we had a lot of fun.

Jay-Z eat your heart out! Getting down with Dennis in a rap for Comic Relief.

... and having a laugh with Frank Bruno during a Fred Olsen sports cruise we both worked on.

Here I am with the great Norman Wisdom...

A lovely picture from the day Jill and I got married in January 2003 at Coombe Abbey, Coventry.

In 2004 I was very proud when Jill graduated having received her Bachelor of Science degree in Human Communication at Demontfort University. It was great dating a student!

Jill and I on TV's *All Star Mr and Mrs*. One of the questions we had to agree on was which one of us was the best looking!

Relaxing at home with Jill along with our cat, Simba, and dogs, Charlie and Alfie.

At 'work' hosting a dinner with Peter Shilton at Leicester City FC. It's been a fantastic and at times traumatic journey, but now I am genuinely happy at home, at work and at play!

did something that I couldn't, but I wouldn't be human if I didn't think about what might have been. If only I could have got past that quarter-final stage in the World Championship during the two years I reached it.

Mind you, I'm not sure Dennis was best pleased with one trip all the Matchroom boys made after he had become world champion in 1985. Barry had set up several different tours for all of us in various countries in the Far East, including Hong Kong and Thailand. It was all part of Barry's trailblazing strategy, and when he did things he did them in style. We travelled first class, stayed in the best hotels and generally had the time of our lives sampling all that the exotic locations had to offer. On this particular trip to Thailand we had the usual huge build-up to our visit in the local media; we were regarded as real stars, and treated as such. We even had to have a police escort from the airport to our hotel, but when we reached the place there was no doubt about who the locals really thought the star of the show was. Written on a huge banner outside was a message: 'Welcome Steve Davis and his colleagues.'

Dennis wasn't too impressed! Not only was he the current world champion, but he had also beaten Steve in dramatic fashion to earn the title.

The fact of the matter was that to so many people at the time, both in Britain and around the world, Steve Davis was snooker. He was the most successful player and as such probably got the most television exposure. Barry had built his Matchroom empire around the fact that Steve was so successful. I suppose in a way we all benefitted from it and I think we realised that, for many people who came to see us play, he was always going to be the star of the show.

Mind you, in years to follow when we played in Thailand, the public's reaction to their first snooker superstar, James Wattana, was amazing. I remember the cheer that went around a hotel in Bangkok, when he beat me 5-4 in the 1995 Thailand Open. It wasn't just from the people who were actually in the arena watching the match, it also came from about 1,000 other people dotted around the hotel who were watching events take place on closed circuit television. I was very much the bad guy, a feeling I used to get whenever I faced Jimmy White or Alex Higgins. It wasn't that the public hated me, it was just that the two of them were such crowd-pleasers and the punters always wanted them to win.

I don't think having Steve as the star of the Matchroom show really caused any problems with the rest of us, because we were part of a group who toured together and had a great time. He certainly wasn't winning everything we were involved with, and all of our profiles were raised during that time. As for Barry, he was never backward in coming forward with new ideas to make sure we remained in the public eye. It was all part of the growth of the game, and it suited all of us. He helped to make us into sporting stars, and with it came the sort of money and fame I would never have believed possible when I first started out as a professional.

CHAPTER EIGHT

SNOOKER LOOPY

Barry Hearn was a natural showman and promoter, but first and foremost he was a very astute businessman with an entrepreneurial instinct for seizing an opportunity. Having seen the popularity of snooker, he set up his Matchroom organisation with a view to creating the sort of product people wanted both in this country and abroad. He did everything with style and with the sort of professionalism that not only made the players feel good, but also projected the right sort of image of snooker to the public and sponsors. He really grasped the potential of the sport, and his impact on the game should not be underestimated.

As for the players who were managed by him in those days, I doubt that any of us had had it so good. There was a tide of enthusiasm for snooker, and we all enjoyed riding the waves.

On a personal level, my profile was probably never higher than in the period from the mid-Eighties to the end of the decade. Losing my hair at a relatively early age had turned out to be a blessing in disguise – the bald head together with the big black moustache became my trademark. At the time, I may not have been the best player in the world, but I was arguably the most recognisable. I was also at my best as a player for a while, and when it came to earning power, the time with Barry Hearn was certainly my best. As ridiculous as it may sound, if you asked me to tell you exactly what I was earning in those days, I couldn't tell you. It was simply a case of knowing that there was a steady flow of money coming through from my snooker playing and everything else which sprang from it.

That first Matchroom tournament showed just how well Barry had set up his organisation. To be able to offer prize money of £50,000 to the winner was incredible really for an invitation-only event, and in doing so he showed the importance of getting corporate sponsorship and television companies involved. He wanted to do everything with a touch of flair, and that's why we always used to travel first class to the far-flung locations around the world that he managed to open up for snooker, places like Dubai, Hong Kong and Thailand.

I used to love travelling around the world in style with Barry and the rest of the boys, but one of my best-ever overseas experiences was not with Matchroom, but with another leading snooker manager Ian Doyle and his Cuemasters organisation when Dennis Taylor and I were asked along as guests.

We used to do the same sort of thing with Matchroom, where Barry would invite another non-Matchroom player or two along for a particular trip in order to make sure there was the right number for a tournament. This particular trip was to New Zealand, and it was only to last for about a week. One of Ian's bright young players at the time was Stephen Hendry, who of course was to go on to become one of the game's greatest-ever players. He was still very good back then but had not quite reached the heights that he would later in his career. We knew we were going to be flying out business class, which was certainly not a bad way to travel, but I had a contact at Heathrow airport who worked in marketing and corporate hospitality. He'd been very good to me in the past, so I phoned him up and told him when we'd be going and asked if there was any chance of us getting an upgrade. I didn't hear anything from him and began to think there wasn't a chance of us being bumped up to the front. However, on the day of the flight, about 10 minutes before we were due to board the plane, a message came over the public address system asking Mr Taylor and Mr Thorne to make themselves known to the airline staff. Sure enough my mate had come up trumps at the eleventh hour and got us our upgrade. By this time the rest of the lads from Cuemasters were waiting at the gate, including Stephen Hendry, who was wearing denims and cowboy boots. We had originally been given blue tickets and baggage tags for our business class flight, but when we got our upgrade these were changed to red. I couldn't resist sticking one of them on my forehead as we walked past our bemused colleagues.

"All right chaps?" I asked as Dennis and I were ushered through and onto the plane.

The two of us were like a couple of giggling schoolboys

when we got to our seats. There we were as guests on the trip with all expenses paid for and we were the ones with the upgrade, not the people who were taking us. Still in naughty schoolboys mode, we couldn't resist composing a letter to the Cuemasters boys, and asked one of the stewardesses to give it to them.

The letter read: 'Dear Mr Doyle and the Cuemasters team, Willie and Dennis would like you to join us in the First Class cabin shortly after take-off. P.s. No denims or cowboy boots!'

After a long but luxurious flight, we landed in Auckland. About ten minutes after I stepped off the plane, Dene O'Kane, New Zealand's best player who reached the quarter-finals of the World Championship in 1987, suggested we hit a few balls. I ended up making a maximum break (something I managed to do in every country I played in abroad). Everything was going my way.

I went on to win the tournament in front of an audience which included the New Zealand Prime Minister and members of the band Simply Red who happened to be on tour in the country at that time. I was feeling pretty pleased with myself as I sat in my hotel room the day after, and an unexpected phone call made me feel even better.

The caller said he'd enjoyed watching me win the tournament and that he was speaking on behalf of the organisers of the Miss New Zealand beauty contest which was being held that night. They knew I would be flying home the following day but wondered if it might be possible for me to be one of the judges. Were they kidding? I'd already had a great week, now I was being invited to judge a beauty contest. Things just seemed to be getting better and better.

I explained to the person on the other end of the line that Dennis Taylor was over with me and eventually managed to wangle an invite for him as well. I thought he'd enjoy himself as much as I intended to do, but to my amazement Dennis declined the offer.

"Thanks, but I've already arranged to go out for a Chinese with the boys," he said. "You go and enjoy yourself, Willie."

I was not only surprised but a bit put out by all of this because Dennis and I had stuck together throughout the trip and we'd had some nice dinners together, including one where we had really pushed the boat out. It was going to cost us an arm and a leg and we were just about to pay, when Ian and the rest of the boys turned up at the same swish restaurant and offered to take care of the bill for us. Ian must have had a real shock because it literally ran into hundreds of pounds!

I was told that the Miss New Zealand organisers said they would send a limousine for me that evening, and I was waiting in reception when the rest of the boys trooped out past me on their way to their Chinese meal. I gave them a smug little grin and waved as I waited patiently for my limo to arrive. I waited for quite a while but there was no sign of a car, and then a taxi driver arrived in reception and explained that he'd been contacted by the limousine company who said that there was a problem with traffic and their car was stuck. They'd asked the taxi firm to pick me up and make sure I got to the contest on time. I was a bit agitated by this, but decided there was nothing I could do about it and jumped into the back of the taxi anticipating a really good night ahead of me.

"Where to?'" the driver asked me.

I told him I didn't have a clue where I was supposed to be going and said that I thought the limo company would have had the sense to fill him in on just where he needed to take me. I went back into the reception area of the hotel and let off steam at the poor guy there, telling him how I needed to get to the beauty contest and that the taxi driver didn't have a clue where he should be going. Eventually the receptionist spoke to the driver and it was sorted out. I climbed back into the taxi, still annoyed by what had gone on, but soon settled back into seat for the ride. After about ten minutes, the taxi pulled over and slowed up in front of a Chinese restaurant, at the front of which was a guard of honour made up of all the lads from Cuemasters, including Dennis!

They had all been in on it – the taxi driver, the receptionist, Dennis and of course all the Cuemasters lads. It was probably particularly sweet for Stephen Hendry after the comment I'd made about his denims and cowboy boots. They had set me up and I had fallen for it. We all had a laugh about it and the whole trip was one I will always remember, because it was such good fun and of course the icing on the cake was the fact that I came back as a winner.

One of the great things about playing snooker abroad was that we always seemed to have a lot of fun. We were there to work and mingle with sponsors, but it was all done in a lovely atmosphere. When you get a group of grown men together in a foreign country you can bet that they will act more like a bunch of kids half the time and that was certainly true during the course of one of the Matchroom trips to Hong Kong.

When we travelled abroad we did so as a group, including Barry who always came with us. Another fixture on these trips was Barry's right-hand man, Robbo. He was always there and would drive Barry around as well as generally being there whenever anything was needed by his boss. Robbo was a real character and all the boys used to love having him around because he was not only a nice guy but also very good entertainment value for the rest of us. He was no spring chicken, but Robbo was always up for anything. When it came to his appearance I have to say that his hairstyle owed more to the Bobby Charlton look, except that, instead of having a few strands spread across his head, Robbo had the full sweep of hair that seemed to start at the back and weave forward to cover his dome. He was probably as bald as me underneath, but his head was so well covered nobody could actually tell, and like me he enjoyed having a bet. Quite often it was a case of feast or famine when it came to his finances, but his personality never really changed and he didn't let the state of his money interfere with his work.

On this particular trip to Hong Kong we all decided to go off on a boat excursion one day when we had some free time. Robbo came along with the rest of the boys and at some stage during the trip somebody bet him that he wouldn't climb the very tall mast of the boat and dive into the sea below. The mast was a big one and I wouldn't even have contemplated going down a slide into the water from that height, but sure enough Robbo was willing to give it a go, much to the surprise of a lot of us. We all watched as he dutifully climbed the thing and waved to us all.

"I'm ready," he shouted down from a great height as we all watched, giggling from the deck of the boat.

Without any warning Robbo then dived off the mast and into the shimmering sea with the rest of us clapping wildly. A few seconds later our clapping became less enthusiastic when we all realised that poor old Robbo had not surfaced, and for a moment I think a few of us thought there might be a problem. But after what seemed to be an awfully long time up he popped out of the water, except this was Robbo as we'd never seen him before.

"I'm alive," he shouted at us, grinning from ear to ear, but it was what was on top of those ears that gave us our biggest laugh. Robbo had surfaced bald headed with his hair, which must have been about three feet long, floating all around him in the sea! The hair was still attached, but instead of being carefully woven on top of his nut, it was now floating around him and the strands seemed to go on forever. It was a hilarious sight, but Robbo didn't care – he was more concerned with the fact that he'd won the bet and taken a few quid off us all.

Hong Kong also brings back happy memories for me because I won a tournament out there that was sponsored by Camus Brandy. It is another example of how Barry was able to put deals together with various sponsors in order to get snooker played in new territories, and the great thing from my point of view was that I knew I was guaranteed money from any of these events. I would pick up perhaps £10,000 for a week's work, and that could be considerably increased if I ended up winning a tournament. Barry's money-making ideas were not just confined to snooker tournaments at home and abroad. He also brought out a range of Matchroom-branded products, from snooker-related items such as chalk and cues to aftershave, pyjamas and slippers.

One of the things we did that is still fondly remembered by many people was to bring out a couple of pop records with Chas 'n Dave. The first, called *Snooker Loopy*, remains the better known of the two and got to number five in the charts when it was released in 1986. We all had a great laugh making the record and the video which went with it. We did the actual recording with Chas 'n Dave at a studio in London and then headed off to the Matchroom offices in Essex for the shooting of the video. One of the verses in the song referred to me and my bald head. 'Old Willie Thorne, he's hair's all gawn,' went the lyric and it ended with the line, 'giving off that glare, perhaps we'll have to chalk it,' and when we were making the video they stuck a load of glitter on my head to make it shine even more than it normally would have done under the lights. The success of that record prompted us to do another, and *The Romford Rap* appeared in the record stores a year later, but didn't do quite so well, only getting to number 48 in the charts. I enjoyed being involved in both of them, but the second of the two also has painful memories for me.

Once again the Matchroom boys had been off to the other side of the world for a tournament, this time in China, and we were due to touch down at Heathrow at about 6am in the morning. It's never easy getting over jet lag following a flight, particularly one which has lasted about 12 hours, so you can imagine how I felt as we all waited by the carousel to collect our bags. In normal circumstances I would have been looking forward to being collected and driven back to Leicester for some rest while my mind and body recovered from the journey, but on this occasion we were all booked to be in the a studio at 9am to film the video that would accompany *The Romford Rap*. It was probably the last thing any of us wanted to do that morning, but once we got there, saw the set and were kitted out in our gear, I think we all really got into it.

The set was fabulous. They had mocked up a giant snooker table on a stage with the cushions all around it about six feet high. All of us players were dressed in the different colours of the snooker balls, and we were asked to stroll along the table with our cues over our shoulders. None of us were exactly in great condition because of the journey we'd just made, but we soon got into the swing of things and everything was going well until I had a little mishap. Just as we were all marching along the stage, I suddenly lost my footing and fell off, missing a work-bench, which had a huge cutting blade attached to it, by inches. I could have badly injured myself but instead ended up with a sore back and a pair of split trousers, exposing my striped underpants to the world. The rest of the lads came running over and asked how I was. They all looked really concerned for me, and it wasn't until later when I watched the footage that I saw them all burst out laughing as soon as I'd had my accident!

We later did a live version of the song at the Hippodrome

in London, but all I could do throughout was sit on the piano, because my back was still sore from the fall I'd had.

I had some great times while I was with the Matchroom organisation. Everything Barry did was top drawer. The other nice thing was that, although all the players had very different characters, we all got on well and I'm sure that helped when we used to go off abroad for days on end. I actually used to find travelling very relaxing. We might have been instantly recognisable to a lot of people in Britain, but often that wasn't the case in some of the countries we visited. We could stroll around and have a laugh and a giggle like any other tourists.

If there was any one of the lads who was a bit like me I suppose it was Jimmy White in that he liked to have a gamble as well. We'd sometimes have challenge matches just between the two of us with the winner maybe picking up £200 or £300 and we would also play cards together. But it never got heavy in any way, it was just a bit of fun for both of us, and we certainly never bet when we played each other in tournaments.

Jimmy was also a similarly instinctive snooker player, and I used to love watching him play simply because of the way he went about his shots. You could learn from him, because he was capable of inventing shots that had never been played before.

One of the lucrative little extras for all of us was playing exhibition matches. You might do these as an individual, but quite often the people organising the event would want two players to come along, which was fine. We would normally each share the workload on the night, but that never seemed to happen with Jimmy, because of who he was and the way he played. He would do all the stuff the crowd wanted during normal frames of snooker and I would have to do all the work afterwards playing set-up trick shots. Part of our job then was to make ourselves available to sponsors who were putting money into the game and getting involved in tournaments and things like exhibitions, but quite often Jimmy would be off straight afterwards leaving other people to make his excuses. It didn't seem to bother people too much, though, and he was as popular as ever and made the game exciting for the public.

Although we worked hard throughout the season, we pretty much had the whole of the summer off because after the World Championship we didn't return to competitive snooker again until September or October. I hardly picked my cue up for two months during the summer. It was a wonderful lifestyle, and everything was taken care of by Barry and his organisation. Barry's skills helped to make all of the Matchroom players into real stars in Britain. We were well known and earned big money, which is all very well if you can handle it properly, but not so great if you are someone like me.

I was still gambling, and was probably betting larger sums than I had ever done in my life, simply because of what I was earning and the potential it then gave me to place bets. I would put bets of £15,000 or £20,000 on at times through the various accounts I had, but when it came to going into a bookmakers I never put more than £2,000 or £3,000 on, simply because they wouldn't accept bigger bets. Whenever you hear stories about someone going into a bookmakers with £50,000 in a bag and putting it all on a horse it makes me laugh, because you just couldn't do that sort of thing.

I was fine with the celebrity bit, and enjoyed that side of it very much. I have already admitted that I am a natural showman who is more than happy to be the centre of attention, but not in a big-headed sort of way. I've always liked the public and they have always liked me. The perception that most people would have had in those days was that we were all rolling in money, and to a large extent they would be right, because there was a lot of cash around. The difference in my case was that I never once thought about saving any of the dough I was earning, and my only investments back then were in the horses I backed, and I backed lots of them.

My trouble was that because of who I was and what I was earning, bookies were more than happy not only to take my money, but also to give me credit. In their eyes I was good for the money because I was well-known, at the top of my game as a professional snooker player. All of this was true and it might not have been too much of a problem if I had wanted a relatively small amount of credit from one bookmaker, but that wasn't the case. I didn't stop at one account; I had lots of them and I didn't just borrow a few bob, I needed serious money with some of the betting I was involved with. It was never a case of betting one big sum, instead I would place several bets of varying amounts, but they would all add up. Throughout my gambling career I don't think I was ever more than £100,000 ahead or more than £100,000 down, but when you start to bet bigger sums it can eventually lead to serious trouble. At first, I had some control, but once I started betting money I didn't physically have, that's when my problems really began.

Of course, I didn't see it like that because I never saw the big picture. I had spent most of my life living for the moment and never thinking or planning for the future. I always thought my career would just go on and on, and I was having such a great time that I just didn't consider what might lie ahead. Nothing and no one goes on forever. I know that now, and if I hadn't been so short sighted and stupid I would have known that then as well.

The saying, 'wake up and smell the coffee,' could not have been more apt. If I had taken time to actually think things through and looked at my life and the way it was going maybe I would have slowed down, or done things differently, but the fact that I wasn't prepared to do it or just didn't think it was important enough says a lot about me. I was always a great one for shutting out things I didn't want to know about. If it was unpleasant or awkward, I avoided it. When I think about that time now, I know I didn't want to take responsibility. I just wanted to have a good time and make the most of the position I found myself in.

Was I being stupid? Yes, of course I was. Life was easy for me. If I wanted money I could earn a lot of it, if I wanted to have a bet with it I would, and when I needed even more to feed my gambling habit I just got credit. I was unaware that I had a gambling problem then, and if anyone had said I had an addiction I would have laughed in their face. It was a bit of fun, just as it always had been, and something that gave me a real buzz.

I realise now that during those heady days I crossed the line, and once I had done that there was no way back for me. There had always been occasions when I bet more money than I should have done, but it had always been relatively controllable. Sure, there were times where I didn't have any cash at all because it had all gone on the horses, but I knew there was another decent payday just around the corner, and I would be able to take care of things, even if it took me a while. I could budget to a certain extent because I knew I would be playing in tournaments, doing tours and taking part in exhibition matches which were very lucrative. There was a stream of outgoings but there was also a pretty constant flow of money coming in.

I had bought a very nice house in one of the best parts of Leicester, called Great Glen, where another famous local lad, Engelbert Humperdinck, also had a home. Both Fiona and I had nice cars, and a few years after the twins were born she gave birth to our daughter, Tahli (a name I'd liked ever since Bruce Grobbelaar had told me that was the name he had given to his daughter). As a family we all had nice clothes and went on nice holidays. With my earning capacity none of this should have been a problem, and in isolation it wasn't. The trouble was that I also had to add another big 'outgoing' to add to all of this, namely, my gambling.

CHAPTER NINE

DEEP POCKETS

My success as a snooker player only helped fuel my betting habit. What had started as a bit of fun and a way of socialising with my pals was now something very different. It was still fun and many of the people who followed me around the various tournaments were still the mates I'd had for years, the same crowd who liked to bet and go to the races. But I was more serious about my betting now, and my contacts within the racing game had grown considerably. I got to know a whole host of other individuals who were well connected in the sport and who were willing to pass on information that might help me get the edge I was always looking for. None of this was crooked; I just got to know people who were well informed.

I was never the sort of gambler who would just have a punt for the sake of it. I paid a lot of attention to the information I got and then made up my mind about who to bet on and how much I wanted to gamble. However, it became obvious that no matter how much information I was getting, I was clearly no professional gambler. I was losing more than I won, but anyone who is a regular with the bookies will tell you that doesn't really change anything. To begin with, if you are totally logical about your life you would never get involved in serious betting, and once you're hooked the fact that you are losing more than you are winning becomes irrelevant, because you only need some wins to blot out the memory of all the disappointment of losing. It's the highs that keep you going, the days when you've had a win or winners, when you feel as though you have beaten the system and come out on top. I had many such highs during the course of my betting life, although I can acknowledge now that I had a lot more lows. You simply don't think about them for too long, because as a gambler you are always looking for the next opportunity, the next horse, the next dog, or the next throw of the dice that will give you the chance to win again. Even when that doesn't happen quickly, or you hit a real losing streak, the gambler's instinct isn't to stop and call it a day. Instead, what happens is that you will often increase your betting in order to try and recoup your losses.

When things really get out of hand and it all seems to be running away from you, when your money is disappearing and you are in debt, that's when you go on the chase, when you desperately keep betting in an attempt to claw some money back in order to give yourself a chance of recovery. In my experience that never happens because by the time that process kicks in you are already too heavily into a way of life that can only ever have one winner and it most definitely is not going to be you.

Throughout my time with Barry Hearn, I was gambling pretty heavily as well as playing snooker for a living. He knew I liked to have a bet and it was certainly no secret within the game that I was a bit of a gambler. The fact that I was a regular at all the racecourses around the country wasn't seen as odd. Lots of well-known sportsmen went racing and it has long been a big hobby with footballers. In fact, some clubs used to take their players to the races as a team-building and bonding exercise. It was a great place for them to let off a bit of steam, have a bet and a laugh and maybe a few drinks as well, before getting on with the more serious business of winning a football match at the weekend.

Although Barry knew I liked to have a bet, there was no way he knew the full extent of my habit during the time I was with him, and why should he? He may have looked after my affairs in as much as I was part of the Matchroom setup, but I was also a grown man and he wasn't there to nursemaid me 24 hours a day. When I was working I did all the things asked of me with regard to playing in tournaments and being available for sponsors who had put money into the events we appeared at. When we went abroad I never really gambled at all. I would have the odd game of cards with Jimmy White and I think we all went dog racing once in Hong Kong, but that was the full extent of my betting habit when I was out of the country.

There was no such thing as internet betting then so you couldn't gamble around the clock as you can do now if you want to, but I just never found the need to keep on gambling once I was abroad and playing snooker. For a start, there were no bookmakers around, but it was also a case of me not really having access to the people and accounts I used when I was back in England. We were also kept busy a lot of the time, not just with the playing of matches, but also with the corporate and sponsorship side of things involved whenever we toured. I used to love being abroad and found it relaxing and enjoyable, so I didn't really miss gambling. Perhaps if I'd spent most of my time abroad I wouldn't have ended up with the problems I did!

These arose from what I did when I was at home, and the fact that I enjoyed horse racing so much. Until recent years, I never really had any appreciation of the value of money. Crazy as that may sound, it's very true, and probably is for many gamblers who have access to some pretty big sums. I might not have had large sums of money in my pocket, but I didn't need to have. The more well known I became, the easier it was to get credit when I wanted and that meant I had even less appreciation of the value of money. All I knew was that if I wanted to go and have a £10,000 bet on a horse, I could. There was never any problem and it meant nothing to me. It was still all about the excitement of betting. Of course, having a big win and collecting my dough at the end of a day's racing was always a lot of fun, and although I've suffered some heavy losses during my life, there have also been wins as well – some big, some small and some which were a bit different.

I loved the life I was leading and I enjoyed nothing more than going to the racetrack whenever I could. I liked the fact that I was a 'face' at the races. I knew lots of people and lots of people knew me. I knew most of the big bookmakers by this time and also a fair few of the private 'layers' who operated at the track. These were people who would often offer better odds, but what they did wasn't exactly legal. Most of them were fine, but you'd have to say that some were not the most scrupulous of people, although they usually paid up if you had a winning bet with them. I remember one guy known as 'The Snake,' who also happened to deal in jewellery as well. He was at Goodwood one day laying bets in his usual fashion and I wanted to back a horse which was being offered as evens by the bookmakers. The Snake said he would give me better odds of 11/10 so I placed my bet with him. The horse won and I went back to collect my winnings – £1,100 – from him, but The Snake was nowhere to be seen. I'd had plenty of bets with him in the past and so I wasn't worried that he'd done a runner. I knew it wouldn't be too long before I saw him again and, sure enough, a few weeks later when I was at the races I spotted him and went to try and collect my winnings, but The Snake was clearly having a few problems.

"Willie, I haven't got the dough," he told me apologetically.

He was a bit short on cash at the time, which was something that often happened to guys like him. The vast majority of them were fine, even if it might take a few weeks for them to get your money for you, but I had heard tales about people in the past putting up an illegal book-making board, taking bets and then clearing off before paying anyone out. The Snake was certainly not like that and it was obvious he wasn't trying it on with me, he just didn't have enough cash.

"I know!" he said, pulling out a load of jewellery from his pocket. "Take this instead. This lot's worth about £1,100."

For all I knew the jewellery might have only been worth £400, but I took it as payment for the debt he owed and had to laugh as he handed it over. Like so many other people who were regulars at the racetracks I went to, The Snake was a character and part of racing's cultural fabric.

One of my favourite courses was Ascot, and one year I had a particularly good time there in the days when you had to collect your winnings from the bookie and be paid in relatively small notes. On this occasion I'd had a very good time and ended up winning more than £40,000 – all in cash. I decided that I'd need some deep pockets in order to stuff the cash into my coat and ended up cutting the lining of the Crombie coat I was wearing in order to make room for storing all the cash. I stuffed money in the pockets and lining of the coat before heading home looking as though I'd put on a few stones during the time I'd been at the course.

As my bets got more extreme, this was something I did on several occasions in order to get all my winnings home with me. When I got back to the house I would empty the cash onto the floor and sit like a kid in a sweet shop as I spread the notes on the carpet and counted the money. Strange as it may seem, I still didn't really have a proper appreciation of the cash that was spread out in front of me, I was a gambler and, as Racing Raymond once told me, "Gambling money is two bob a bucketful". By that he meant that it's just a way of betting more. You're not going to use it for anything other than betting and therefore it loses its real value for you. If I had taken my winnings and said, "Right, I'm going to buy a new car with this," it would have been a bit different, but whenever I looked at that amount of cash I really only saw it as a way of going out and betting again. The pound notes were like chips in a casino, they just allowed me to carry on doing what I liked best – having a bet.

Of course, it was great to have cash and not have any worries about spending some dough, but the real excitement for me was in beating the system, pulling off a bit of a coup. It was more about fun than money, probably because snooker was bringing me plenty of the latter at the time. I was at the peak of my earning powers and in 1987 I ended up a huge winner financially, despite losing out to Steve Davis in a big tournament.

In 1986, I had reached the final of the Irish Masters in Dublin but eventually came unstuck against Jimmy White who beat me 9-5. A year later, I was back at the Masters and once again went on a winning run which took me all the way to the final, this time against Steve Davis. I had bet on myself all the way in the previous rounds and had already made about £40,000 in the process. I felt good and I felt lucky, so I wanted to put everything I had already won on beating Davis in the final. But at the time there was no such thing as Sunday betting and so I wasn't able to put any money on myself. This turned out to be a blessing in disguise, because Steve beat me 9-1, and I would have lost the lot. Instead, I kept my winnings and also had the added bonus of picking up about £25,000 as the losing finalist, so I was more than £60,000 better off. But it didn't stop there. I had also been given very good tips on some horses that had been running throughout the week of the tournament at various courses. My sources really came up trumps and by the time I walked out to face Davis, I had won around £60,000 in bets. It was incredible. I might not have won the Masters, but there was definitely a silver lining for me as I returned to England about £120,000 better off, most of which was once again stuffed in the reliable old Crombie I was wearing.

When I got back to Manchester I went straight to the house of David Taylor, aka 'The Silver Fox', a former World Amateur Snooker champion who never quite reached the same heights as a professional. We used to get on well and when I arrived at his place, I carried out my usual post-winning ritual of spreading all the cash out on the carpet in front of me before counting it. I even asked David if he wanted any cash as a loan and ended up handing him £7,000 for a dining room suite, which was helpful for him and also for me, because it relieved some of the weight I was carrying in the lining of my coat!

Instances like that were wonderful, but the reality was that a huge win had to be balanced against all the losses I suffered over a number of years.

The biggest single win I ever had was £38,000. The others might have been more profitable wins overall, but they were as a consequence of making several bets in order to try and win some big money. I once did this very successfully and I happened to have a very personal interest in the horse I was backing because I part-owned it. I had gone into the partnership with my professional gambling pal, 'Ginger Steve', along with the comedian and actor, Mel Smith. I was involved with a few horses during the 1980s, but it was a particular one called Treasure's Jubilee, which I still recall with great fondness, because not only did it win me a lot of money from just one race, it also gave me one of my best-ever moments on a racecourse.

Steve contacted me one day and said that he'd heard about a horse which was trained at stables in North Wales and was convinced that buying it could lead to us all making a substantial amount of money. The plot was pretty simple: he'd heard that the horse had something about it and could be a winner, but it hadn't run for a while because of an injury to one of its legs which was very badly swollen. Although it had won the previous season, that was one of only two wins in its entire career. Undeterred by this lack of form, Steve was convinced it would make a good investment for the three of us and asked me if I could make the trip to Wales and have a look at the horse. It was being kept at a yard run by a woman called Cathy Lloyd-Jones. When I went up there to see her and the horse she did a pretty convincing job of telling me that, despite the way Treasure's Jubilee looked, it had great potential once it was over the injury. She said it had genuine class, but when I saw it for myself I had doubts. It looked terrible and certainly showed no signs that it might be a potential winner for us, but Cathy insisted it was a great opportunity because Treasure's was a horse with real ability. She also pointed out that when it did eventually race again, the fact that it had been away for so long would probably see it start with a very favourable price, giving us the chance to cash in on the odds it would attract.

In the end she convinced me it would be a decent investment and I agreed that we would buy the horse for £5,000. Once we had decided to take it, the next part of the plot was to ensure the horse was entered in the right sort of race when it next ran. Steve was a very methodical man, just as you would expect from someone who earned their living as a professional gambler. He did his homework and went about things very professionally, aiming to give himself the best possible chance of succeeding, so once we'd bought Treasure's Jubilee, he took a keen interest in the progress it was making following the injury. Steve went up to North Wales and watched Treasure's Jubilee on the gallops, checking its progress to see exactly when he thought it would have the best chance of success in a race.

We decided that the race we were looking for was a two-mile hurdle at Ludlow. The favourite for the race was a horse trained by Martin Pipe, and although we owned Treasure's Jubilee we kept it registered in Cathy's name because having a celebrity name attached to a horse will get more people putting money on it and that, in turn, will affect the starting price. By the time the day of the race arrived I had put on about £12,000, placing small bets on the horse all around the country using people I knew through racing. Once again, the reason for this was all to do with the pricing of the betting for Treasure's Jubilee. Putting on small amounts was less likely to attract attention in the way a big bet would have done in terms of bringing down the price. I was like a little kid on the day of the race and, even though Steve had suggested that I stay away from the course, I couldn't resist the temptation to go to Ludlow and watch for myself.

I got recognised by a few people at the course who wondered what I was doing there, and it all became a bit of a cloak-and-dagger operation for me as I tried to be careful about the way I actually bet at the course. I would have loved to have put a very large bet on, but I knew I had to show a bit of restraint, so instead put just £100 on it at 12/1. By the time the race started its odds had come down to 8/1, which was still pretty good, particularly if it managed to perform in the way that Cathy believed it could. Martin Pipe's favourite was about 20 lengths clear of the five other horses in the race in the first mile, but Treasure's Jubilee began to show its class by working its way through the field to make sure it was in contention coming into the home straight. With three hurdles to jump, it was gaining on the leader and my heart was beating like a drum.

It's always great cheering on the horse you've bet on, but this wasn't any old horse or any old bet for that matter. This was a horse I now part-owned, and over a long period of time I had carefully placed bets on it which could now see the three of us winning in the region of £100,000. With two of the hurdles to go, it went to the front and I could hardly contain myself. I was trying to look reasonably composed, but my emotions were going through the roof. It was an unbelievable feeling, like nothing else I had experienced before at a racetrack. The whole scheme was about to come to fruition if Treasure's Jubilee went past that winning post first. We had bought the horse, waited for it to recover from the injury we knew it had, and then entered it in a race we believed it had the potential to do well in. Not only had it done well, it was about to win and I was about to make a substantial amount of money.

As the horse went over the line I felt like jumping in the air, but somehow I stopped myself from doing so. I couldn't have been happier or more contented with life during that split second when I realised that Treasure's Jubilee was the winner. The money was great, but it was more than that. I suppose it had a lot to do with that old feeling which I never tired of, that feeling of beating the system. Nobody really gave us a chance of a win and the betting reflected that, but we knew the potential of the horse and backed our judgement. I later went over to collect my winnings from the bet I'd had at the course, and after congratulating Cathy and thanking her for all the work she had put in I sauntered over to my car for the drive back to Leicester. On the way home I couldn't stop smiling at what had happened and the fact that I was going to pocket some very decent dough as a consequence. To this day it remains one of my happiest-ever racing memories.

That win at Ludlow was a very good example of having the sort of edge I was always looking for when I had a bet. It certainly didn't work all of the time, though, and even the Ludlow race could have blown up in our faces. With all the information we had on the horse and the fact that I was able to place so many different little bets around the country, ultimately, it was still a gamble, but that risk factor is something that someone like me has always found attractive. It's the idea that, despite it all being a gamble, you believe you can make it work and you're willing to risk your money in order to try and come out a winner. That gambling instinct also spilled over into the way I would sometimes approach my snooker. I would take risks and go for shots that maybe I should not have. Sometimes it worked, but often it didn't.

I'm sure a lot of people will consider what I have done in my life to be completely insane; it is certainly illogical when you think of what I had going for me. They will see that I earned well as a snooker player and then ask why I wanted to risk it all by having a bet. The reason is that although I had a great life I suppose I always wanted something better and maybe I saw gambling as a quick way of making the sort of money that would enable me to have that. It is also true to say that I was just hooked on having a bet, of taking on the system, of beating the odds and, once I had become so immersed in the gambling culture, I found it very difficult to break away and end my involvement. Horse racing was always my preferred gambling avenue, but that didn't mean I was averse to other forms of betting. Although I was never a particularly heavy hitter when it came to casinos, I always loved going to them for a night out. They were very different places to the racecourse and you could see an awful lot of money being gambled on the roll of some dice or the turn of a card.

There was something about a casino that I found hugely seductive. For a start they had an air of class and sophistication about them. People were usually dressed well and they didn't just offer gambling, but also the chance to eat really good food in lovely restaurants. I suppose you should realise you're going to come off second best when your feet sink into their carpets, but it never stopped me going to them. For a time I enjoyed going even more when I had the good fortune to meet someone who was able to give me the sort of edge in casinos that I was always looking for with the horses. His name was Richard Olsen and he was best known for his skill as a backgammon player.

The snooker club I had opened in Leicester continued to do well and one of the games we often used to play for fun was backgammon. We had some pretty good players in there, but one guy stood out from all the rest and we quickly realised that he was a very good player indeed. Backgammon is a great game, but there are varying levels when it comes to the people who play it, and there's a lot of skill involved. It may involve throwing dice, so in that sense you could say there is an element of luck, but then a player has to be very strategic in the way they go about playing the game. The guy who came into my club was clearly a cut above anyone else around, and it wasn't long before he was using his ability in casinos, where the game was a big feature during the 1980s.

When you played backgammon for money it was all about how much was going to be wagered on each point. So, for example, playing for £20 a point could see a player win or lose about £2,000 or £3,000 on a game. Once we'd seen how good the guy was it was obvious some money could be made from getting him to play in casinos, so that is exactly what we did. One trip we made with him was to a casino in Birmingham where he played a game against a really big guy who looked and sounded pretty confident.

The stake was £20 a point and it became obvious that although our man was good, the big guy was even better. He knew who I was and at one point during the course of the game he leaned across to have a quiet word in my ear.

"Look Willie," he said in a very friendly voice. "I like you, so that's why I'm telling you that this kid can't beat me. Don't get me wrong, he can play and he's good, but he's not good enough."

He was right and I could only look on and marvel at the fact that I was watching someone who was seriously good at playing backgammon. That was my introduction to Richard Olsen, and from that day the two of us became good friends. I later discovered that Richard was one of the best backgammon players in the world, but one of his other great skills was being able to card count, something that gave me just the sort of edge I was looking for when I went to a casino. I found out that most backgammon players also liked to play cards and Richard was no exception, but it was his ability as a card counter which really set him apart. It was incredible to watch him in action when it came to something like blackjack. I could count up to a point but nothing like Richard and I couldn't do the ace game like him either. He would watch the shuffle and then know pretty much where the ace was. He would be talking to me and say things like, "The Queen of Spades will come out in the next four or five cards – when that happens there'll be four aces in the next seven cards." Sure enough the Queen of Spades would then pop up and then all of a sudden the four aces would come out in the next seven cards.

It was amazing to watch him in action, and I would often act as his stooge or front man. This would mean me causing a bit of a distraction around the table by talking to people, but we weren't doing anything illegal or dishonest. Richard basically had a skill and we were exploiting it. When he felt the odds were in our favour and knew the cards were going to come out, we would start to bet £400 per box instead of the £25 we'd been having.

Of course, it didn't always work out to our advantage because the dealer would sometimes get an ace, in which case our odds of cleaning up suddenly diminished, but we had some very good nights. I never won anything like I did at the races – I think the most I probably ever won in one night in a casino was about £20,000, which is not to be sniffed at, but by the time I had teamed up with Richard I was earning pretty good money from my snooker. I didn't need the money from the casino betting as I might have done in later years, but I loved the buzz I got from beating the system. Obviously casinos didn't like having card counters like Richard around and they latched onto the fact that cutting cards thinly as they used to made it easier for them to count, so they began to cut off two and a half or three packs out of a total of six, making the whole thing virtually impossible to count.

Watching Richard play backgammon was also an education, and I was lucky enough to go and see him compete in World Championships a couple of times. The competition took place at a grand hotel in Monte Carlo with four huge rooms being used to house the players. It was a major event, played in a luxurious setting and the prize money was something like £25,000. Richard enjoyed competing in the big events like that just as anyone with his ability would do, but there was one game I fixed up for him for even bigger money which was in marked contrast to the surroundings he was accustomed to in Monte Carlo.

Every year just after the snooker World Championship at the Crucible I used to head off to the Pontins tournament held at one of their holiday camps at Prestatyn in north Wales. It was always an event I looked forward to, and I had won the Spring Open tournament in 1980 with that win over Cliff Wilson and also had the victory in the Pontins Professional event against John Spencer in 1984. On this particular occasion I heard about somebody who was in town for the snooker, but who was also eager to play backgammon against anyone for £100 a point, which could mean winning or losing £50,000. It was a huge amount to gamble and the guy seemed pretty confident in his own ability, but not as confident as I was in my belief that Richard would be able to beat him. So I phoned Richard who was in London at the time and asked him what he was doing the next day.

"Where are you, Willie?" he asked me.

"I'm in Prestatyn, Richard," I told him.

Stunned silence on the other end of the phone. He was clearly not impressed with the thought of travelling all the way to north Wales, but when I told him how much the guy wanted to wager he became interested. I told Richard the other player came from Manchester and was reckoned to be the best in the city. Undeterred by this, Richard told me to agree to the game and made his way up to Wales, having to change trains about six times in the process. He finally arrived looking as well dressed as ever in a beautifully tailored suit, lovely shirt and handmade shoes. Richard looked every inch the successful backgammon player and there was a real air of confidence as he went about his work. After about three hours play there was a break and he gave me his verdict on the man from Manchester.

"He's good Willie," Richard admitted. "But don't worry I'll beat him and get the money."

Sure enough, that's exactly what happened, Richard was just too good and, although it took a while, the bag of cash our friend from Manchester had brought along ended up in the hands of Richard, making his trip to Wales very worthwhile.

I had a lot of gambling contacts by this time, not just bookies or trainers in the racing world, but other people who were generally part of the scene. One of these was a guy from London called Mick who rang me one day and asked about the possibility of arranging a backgammon game with Richard for some high stakes. He said he had someone called Harold coming over from America who was a really good player and a professional gambler. The stakes were going to be high with Richard and I sharing the cost of the betting on each point, and the game was going to take place in Leicester.

We managed to find out a bit more about our mystery guest from the States, and the information we got wasn't good. He might have been a professional gambler, but the information that came back to us was that he was also a cheat with the remarkable ability to throw the dice using the kind of trick a magician would have been proud of. In effect he could rattle the dice while holding on to one of them and then let them drop, making it look as though everything had been done correctly. What he was actually doing was reducing the odds because one of the dice would conveniently drop with the number he wanted, while the other was left to chance. It was brilliant, and unless you knew about it there was no way you could ever have guessed what was going on. We also found out that that he'd used things like weighted dice in the past, with magnets under the backgammon board so that, thrown in the correct way, he could once again get the sort of numbers he wanted. If we were going to make the game, we decided it would have to be on terms that we'd be happy with. That meant playing with a board which we would provide and, as an extra precaution against the possibility of him cheating, I would be the person throwing the dice for Harold.

When all of this was suggested to him it was agreed and he must have realised we'd done our homework, but he still had enough confidence in his own ability to agree to the game taking place in the way we had suggested. He proved to be a very good player; indeed, he was probably one of the best in the world and Richard found it really tough against him. After about four hours, the game was going nowhere and we called it a day, but by that time we had at least managed to get a few thousand pounds off him.

I think there was a lot of mutual respect between Richard and Harold for the way they could both play backgammon. Neither of us liked the fact that when the game had first been suggested, Harold was clearly looking to cheat his way to some money, but we chatted to him after the game and I have to admit he was quite a character.

He was clearly a very clever man, but also crooked. He'd apparently travelled around Europe leaving a trail of deception and at the same time winning lots of money, but his gambling brought him into contact with some heavy people. He must have won money off the wrong sort of people, because he had been chased around the continent by a few unsavoury figures, before managing to hitch up in Leicester. Don't ask me how it happened, but at least we didn't become two more of his victims.

Harold clearly loved to gamble, but it seemed to me that he liked to cheat almost as much. I was always looking to win when I had a bet, but there was never a time when I resorted to out and out cheating or did anything illegal. Of course, I liked to have an edge so I was always looking for useful information before I had a bet, but there was one particular occasion when the opportunity to get involved in a gambling coup took on a new and sinister meaning for me.

I know that over the years there have been people who have claimed match-fixing goes on in snooker. Let me say right now that apart from a few isolated cases which have been exposed and dealt with by the governing body, snooker could not be cleaner. But it would be naive and wrong of me to claim the sport has always been immune from the occasional attempt to influence a result. In 1995, South African Peter Francisco was involved in a scandal at the World Championships when he played Jimmy White and lost 10-2. A lot of money had been placed on that score, so much so that betting was suspended shortly before the match started. There was no wrongdoing on Jimmy's part, but Francisco was banned for five years. And in 2006 Australian Quinten Hann was banned for eight years and fined £10,000 when he was found guilty of agreeing to lose a match to Ken Doherty (completely unbeknown to Ken). More recently, John Higgins found himself embroiled in a tabloid sting instigated by the *News of The World* newspaper, receiving a six-month ban after an investigation found he had failed to report an invitation to breach the sport's betting rules – I hasten to add, that an independent tribunal found John completely innocent of match-fixing.

These were high-profile cases, but happily they are rare examples in the sport. However, the fact remains that there will always be some individuals who will try to influence things like sporting contests, simply because there is money to be made from it. There have been similar allegations in sports like cricket and football, with betting syndicates in far-flung places supposedly trying to influence the outcome of matches.

I am not sure whether it was because I was well known for my gambling or whether some people just thought I might be an easy touch and would go along with their suggestion in order to make a bit of extra cash, but I was once approached in a hotel by an individual who wanted to know if I would fix a match I was due to play against Joe Johnson. He wanted me to make sure I lost to Joe and in return I would be given £20,000. At first I wasn't sure whether he was serious, but it pretty quickly became apparent that he was and I just as quickly turned the offer down.

"Willie, there's £20,000 in it for you," he said, obviously thinking the sum would be too much for me to resist.

"I don't care if you offered me £100,000, I'm not interested," I told him.

I think he realised there was no chance of me changing my mind simply because of the way I'd replied to him, and he didn't try to persuade me to think again, or threaten me in any way. I was clean and there was no way I was going to turn crooked.

I know I was probably the biggest gambler on the snooker circuit and I'm sure whoever the guy was probably knew that, and as such maybe thought I was more likely to go along with the scheme. Not only would I have got some money from him, but I'm sure he thought I would have taken advantage of various bets to make sure I came out with a decent amount of cash from the whole thing. The truth is this guy's attempt to get at me never got off the ground and I never saw him again.

I never reported the incident at the time it happened – once I'd turned him down I considered the matter closed so I never thought about the need to report it. I also wanted to deal with the whole thing in the best way possible and that was by beating Joe Johnson, which was exactly what I went on to do.

Thankfully I never had to deal with such a problem again. The biggest problems I had to deal with were all self-inflicted caused by a gambling habit that was lurching out of control.

CHAPTER TEN

ADDICTED

Although the late Eighties should have been some of the best years of my life, they turned out to be some of the most painful and difficult I have ever experienced. The public image I presented was of someone who had everything under control and was enjoying the fruits of being a top-earning sportsman. In private, I began to see my life unravelling before my eyes.

I wasn't aware of what was happening at first. I carried on in much the same way as I had always done: playing snooker, betting on the horses and generally having a pretty good time. When you gamble, the very nature of what you are doing means there are no guarantees about winning. In fact, more often than not you are likely to be a loser. It's all part of the game and you accept it because there is always that possibility of turning things around with your next bet. Even if I lost a lot of money, I was soon on to the next horse believing the bet would turn things around for me, and quite often that was exactly what happened. You win some, you lose some, or so the saying goes, but when you lose some and then lose some more, things start to take on a new and more sinister look.

My problems really escalated when I started making big bets using credit. I was never the sort of person who kept track of what I was betting and how much I was losing. I tended to live for the day and not worry about anything long-term. If there was a problem I was the sort of person who believed it would sort itself out without me really having to do anything about it, but when I hit a bad losing streak that all changed. It began to dawn on me that I had spent money I didn't have, and because I wasn't winning there was no real way of paying off the large amounts.

Fiona knew I gambled, and we both used to enjoy the good times when I would come home from a racecourse with huge amounts of money which I would spread out on the carpet. It allowed us to have a great lifestyle and be able to afford lots of luxuries other couples might only have dreamed about, but when things started to go wrong for me she was unaware of what was happening. There was no way she could have realised because I was very secretive about the amounts I was betting, and she never got to see the post which showed the sums I owed in the various accounts I had at the time. I was in a downward spiral financially but she never got to know about the full extent of it, and neither did anyone else, until it was too late.

I had never been the kind of gambler who was always desperate to have a bet. I used to put my money on horses which I thought had a really good chance, based on infor-mation from people I trusted as good judges with knowledge about what was going on in the racing world, but the more

I lost, the more I needed to try and get myself back to winning ways. I had been careful about covering my tracks and, like most gamblers, I became very devious in the way that I went about things in order to keep the full extent of my problems a secret.

My fame and celebrity allowed me to take the extra step when I entered a new phase in my gambling addiction – namely, the world of credit betting. The consequences of this would go on to blight my life for many years to come. I was able to start using all the different accounts I had opened up to bet. At first, it wasn't a case of me spending money I didn't have, it was just a way of being able to place bigger bets and to do it without physically having to pull up the money. I was still earning enough to be able to cover a lot of this gambling, but the longer it went on the more out of control it became.

The other problem was that I was slowly but surely slipping down the snooker rankings. I did reach number seven in the world again in 1993, but two seasons later I dropped out of the elite top 16 and once things began to slide there was no way of reversing the trend. It was something I had never contemplated; lots of sportsmen don't.

Nobody, no matter who they are and how good they are, can stay at the top of their sport forever. I was never the best snooker player in the world, but I was certainly one of the best. I was blessed with natural ability, and it allowed me to have a good career and a lot of fun, but it had to end. That is the one certain thing for anyone involved in professional sport, and it was something I never fully grasped until it was all too late. To have so much going for me and to screw it all up is not a pleasant thing to have to admit, but there is no other conclusion I can come to. I might have been in the middle of an addiction I had failed to recognise, but I still think I knew what I was doing to a large extent and how much it was having an impact on my life. It eventually proved costly in more ways than one. I was well on the road to financial ruin, and I was also about to enter a period of my life that would tear my young family apart.

I now realise that I was addicted to gambling. I am making no excuses for the way I carried on and the trouble I got myself into. I have nobody else to blame but myself, and I am certainly not looking for sympathy, but I do sometimes wonder what I would have done had I not been able to get the credit I did. I'm sure it wouldn't have stopped me betting, but it would have made it more difficult for me. To physically pull out money from your pocket is a very different matter to phoning up and getting money on a horse. Credit betting was all too easy for me.

I can't blame the bookies – they were just doing their job. They saw me parading around racecourses and playing snooker on television, so they knew I was good for a few bob. That was true and my betting might not have got out of hand if I had restricted myself to one or two accounts and then kept the amounts I was gambling in check, but at one time I must have had 15 or even 20 different accounts, of which five or six would have been at the track. The others would be phone accounts, a form of betting that made it all too easy for me to fritter away sums of money I didn't actually have. Maybe some of it was bravado, I really don't know. What I do know is that even if I only intended having a £1,000 phone bet, by the time I dialled the number I was thinking of having £5,000 and when I actually spoke that amount would often be increased to £10,000. This sort of betting was not a one-off thing with me. The amounts might have varied and they certainly weren't all big bets, but the pattern was the same. It was all numbers, all multiples, and none of them really meant anything to me. I would still only bet on horses that I'd been given information about, but once I started to hit a losing streak my betting pattern began to change.

It is what is known as 'the chase', where you go chasing after money by placing bets on all sorts, and with whatever dough you can lay your hands on in the hope of catching up and getting back the cash that you have lost. All gamblers take risks but when you get to this stage the risks become that much bigger. I would sometimes put huge sums on horses in the hope of getting some money, but it never worked. Instead I just got myself in deeper trouble. I began to keep a little book with details of the accounts I had and how much was in each. If I owed a lot in one and then had a win with another, I would transfer some of the winnings over to the account that was in trouble in order to make sure it was kept open and I could keep using it. I became a master at switching different sums from one account to another in an effort to keep them open and functioning, hoping that somewhere along the line the losing streak would end and I would begin to get myself ahead of the game.

When you're in that sort of position you will try almost anything to get out of it and the trouble was that, even if

I did have the odd win or two, they still weren't enough to get me out of the hole I had dug for myself. It was the overall trend that was really hurting me and I started to feel the pressure. During the late Eighties and early Nineties I was still playing snooker and trying to maintain a successful career, but the pressure was such that at times I went into tournaments knowing I needed to get to the quarter-finals because I so desperately needed the money. I can even remember playing in an event and trying to find out what had won the 2.30 at one of the courses that day. I did this by relying on snooker's famous MC, Alan Hughes. He would stand in the wings and if I'd told him I had a bet on he would find out who won the race and then give me the thumbs up or thumbs down.

My money troubles were making me more and more moody at home. I would snap at the least little thing and lie awake at night worrying about how I was going to get out of the mess I was in. I suppose I became more and more withdrawn from Fiona and my family. She didn't know about the mounting bills and the various book-making accounts I had and was shuffling around as I tried to keep my head above water. I still found it difficult to fully understand what was happening and just kept believing that the next bet would be the one to reverse the trend. I suppose I was in denial. I kept putting off the reality of my situation, hoping it would all go away, but I had set something in motion that had got out of control and I had no way of putting the brakes on.

It must be very difficult for people to understand how I managed to get myself into such a mess, taking into account all I had going for me in my life, but it really didn't matter what I had or what I did. I was a gambler and as such my thoughts and actions were completely different to those of most people. I had a different kind of mindset. I didn't do the normal things other people do, and I certainly wasn't sensible when it came to money. If I had been I would never have started betting in the way that I did. I know lots of people will have a bet on a regular basis and go horse racing without ever getting near to the situation I was in, but that's the difference between being a gambler, or rather someone who enjoys gambling, and being addicted. It's the difference between someone having a couple of pints in a pub, and someone who goes home and polishes off a bottle of whisky. One can handle it, the other can't, and as such becomes a slave to their addiction.

There are no reasons I can put forward to explain the way I acted. Whether it was something in me that was triggered by the excitement I got from having a bet, or whether I was always destined to have an addictive personality, I don't really know. Some may say that I had more money than sense and in a way that would be right. I certainly had a decent amount of money to fund my habit and, of course, what I did made no sense at all, but you don't have to be earning big money to become addicted to gambling. I'm sure there are lots of people who have had a terrible time because they couldn't stop betting, and they wouldn't have earned anything like the money I did during my snooker career. There are no specific types of people who are susceptible to the gambling bug, it goes right across the board and through all social classes of our society. What

I would say as someone who was once a high-earning sportsman is that I think there are some people within sport who are perhaps more prone to getting involved in betting, simply because of the nature of what they do.

A prime example of this would be footballers who have long been known to like a bet on the horses or get involved in card schools on the way to and from matches, although I understand this is less a part of the match day ritual as it used to be. The fact is that footballers have always had a lot of time on their hands. During the week they will train for maybe four mornings and then have the afternoons free. The gambling troubles of Matthew Etherington have been well documented – and happily he has overcome them – but I very much doubt he is an isolated case. Paul Merson is another footballer who has admitted that he bet heavily during his playing career, and his gambling addiction became a huge problem. He loved to bet and, unlike me, would have a gamble on pretty much anything. It is only people like Matthew, Paul and I who can really begin to understand what a grip gambling can take on your life, and that's why I believe there are probably Premier League footballers out there today, who are at the top of their game professionally and seem to have it all, but who are in fact dangerously out of control.

It is a myth to believe that because a footballer might be earning £100,000 a week he has enough money to bet and not to worry about it. The perception is that he is swimming in cash and can afford pretty much everything he wants, which to a large extent is true. If he wants a brand new sports car that costs the equivalent of a couple of week's wages, it really isn't going to affect his bank balance or his lifestyle that much, and if he wants to go out and buy a huge house, that is easily affordable as well. So if he wants to spend some money betting on the horses or the dogs, he has the dough to do so without really missing it, but as I have mentioned, when it comes to having a bet, it is all a question of multiples.

By that I mean that if an ordinary working man earning, say, £300 a week goes out and has a £10 bet each week and sticks to that amount, it's probably fair to say that it won't affect his lifestyle too much and he can afford to do it without any harm coming to him or his family. But suppose that same man decides that instead of sticking to his £10 bet, he wants to lay down more money. He might start at £20 or £50 and then get the taste for it, so he moves on and begins to bet bigger and bigger. If he's not careful he could pretty soon be gambling a huge chunk of his weekly wage.

It would be no different for a top footballer. Say he earns £100,000 a week after tax and bets £10,000 or even £20,000 of that it probably won't really affect him. It might be a huge sum to most people, but in relative terms he can afford to do it if he wants to. But if those bets escalate to £75,000 or £90,000 of that weekly wage he will soon be in trouble. It's not beyond the realms of possibility that he could end up betting all of what he earns, or worse still getting into the problem of betting what he doesn't actually have. I know it may sound crazy, but it isn't, believe me. The point is that it doesn't matter how much money you earn or how much money you have, if you are addicted to gambling it can all

ADDICTED

start to disappear very quickly. Having money doesn't protect you from going broke and it can actually be very dangerous. If a footballer has big money coming in on a regular basis throughout his career at the top, it is very easy for him to believe that things will stay the same and go on forever. I certainly used to feel like that when I was playing snooker, but that just isn't the case for anyone in sport.

Sooner or later your powers start to deteriorate, and with that comes a drop in your earning power. If a Premier League player has been sensible and looked after his money, he will be set up for life, but if he has been gambling for a large part of his career then that certainly won't be the case. What happens when the £100,000 a week goes down to £50,000 or £25,000 or £10,000? All huge sums to most people but if so much of the money he has earned has been gambled away, the problems that would bring are obvious. I never earned anything like the vast sums that some footballers do these days, but in relative terms I did gross an awful lot of money in my career, particularly when I was at my peak. That should have set me up for life without having to worry about money, but it didn't. There was no logic in what I did, but there was a need to keep doing it no matter what happened. Whether it was me, a working-class guy earning a few hundred pounds each week, or a high-earning foot-baller, the pitfalls of gambling are there for anyone.

Taking that first step and having a bet for fun may seem harmless enough, and probably is for the vast majority of people, but there will be others, people like me, for whom having a casual bet just isn't enough and they are the ones who are most vulnerable. The real problem is recognising the dangerous road they are travelling on and doing something about it before it becomes too late and they find themselves in a mess. It's always easy to persuade yourself that it couldn't happen to you, that everything is alright and under control, but when you start telling yourself that is the case, the opposite is probably true and you are already way out of control.

I never believed I would have a problem financially from my betting other than the odd loss here and there, but I couldn't have been more wrong. In the end the need to gamble takes over, and the ease with which I could do that because of being able to get credit, was frightening. It has never been easier than it is these days to bet or to get credit to bet, particularly if you are a high earner. To compound that fact, having large amounts of money often makes you very careless. You lose all sense of reality, until you realise your betting has become a problem. By then, it is usually too late to be able to correct the trend, and that's when you begin to become desperate as you try to recoup your losses. You start to chase the money you need and any logic that might have been used in the past goes out of the window. It's all about trying different bets, hoping they will come off and give you what is needed, but it never happens.

When gambling gets a grip you become a different kind of person, or at least that was true in my case. I was still able to maintain a façade which suggested everything was normal – in public I was very much the same as I'd always been. I managed to have a smile on my face when I needed to and would have a laugh and a joke with people. But in my more private moments it was a very different matter.

I would sit and worry about my situation and then try and plot a way out, which inevitably involved me trying to get the sort of tips and information that would lead to being able to back a winning horse. A gambler's psyche is very different to any normal person because no matter how bad things have been or how terrible they are at any given moment, you always think to yourself 'Today's the day,' and you go off and start betting again. When I was in a hole I used to think, 'I'll go out and win £10,000 today and then if I get another £10,000 tomorrow things are starting to look better,' but I was just kidding myself because it never happened and everything went from bad to worse.

The weird thing is how the ability to bet is like a huge adrenalin rush to the system; it's as if someone has given you a powerful injection that has lifted your spirits. When I was on my losing streak, if someone had given me £5,000 to help me out, my first thought wouldn't have been to put it towards paying off my debts, it would have been to put the money on a horse. I would be thinking that I could use the £5,000 and turn it into £25,000 or £30,000 by having a bet, rather than thinking that if I used the money to have a bet I could be blowing the lot and seeing nothing in return. As a consequence of this and the way I operated, I would regularly blow any spare cash I had. Just having the money to gamble would make me excited at the prospect of what it could bring, the possibility of turning £1,000 into £10,000 in the space of a few minutes. So in many ways, although I had some very dark moments, it was never all doom and gloom when there was always the possibility of being able to gamble.

Once I got a sniff of some cash or the possibility of credit it gave me a lift. From being down on the floor mentally I suddenly started to fantasise about winning even before the race had been run, and my mind would go into overdrive about what it would allow me to do next. It was never really about being able to sort out any kind of mess I was in, it was more about being able to carry on gambling.

Although I never really appreciated the value of money, that doesn't mean to say I didn't care if I had any or not. I always wanted money and loved the luxuries of life it gave me. But because I felt I would be able to have lots of it thanks to my playing career and my gambling, I never treated it with the respect I should have and never used it in the right way. I realise that now, many years after all of my problems began to surface, but at the time I was too engrossed in a lifestyle that had always involved betting. It was what I did, just as much as playing snooker was.

I wish now that I had never ever started to have a bet, that I could have been like so many other people and not been interested at all. I just wish I knew why I had a need to gamble. It was something in me, part of what I was about. It probably also had an effect on the way I went about my snooker. I did probably take more risks than I should have, but the other side of that is that perhaps the gambler in me made my game more exciting to watch. Sometimes even I was surprised by some of the shots I opted to take on. It was just something in my make-up.

I had started out loving the buzz of cheering on a horse from the stands as it galloped into the home straight, and I still loved watching the horse I'd backed romp home, but things had moved on from there. Although it was me who physically put money on and chose the bets I was going to have, I had really gone past the point of thinking about what I was doing. It was almost as if something within me was leading me to do all of this, even though I knew deep down that it was going to end in tears.

There was a lot of strain on my professional career as a snooker player because of the money worries I had. I even used the money I got for exhibitions to have a bet. I might earn two or three thousand pounds for one evening's work and then blow the lot on gambling. There was also added pressure when I played in tournaments because now I desperately needed to try and reach the quarter-finals and get the £8,000 or £10,000 it would guarantee. I'm not sure I was any less confident as a player, just more aware of the fact that I needed the money and I suppose that must have had some effect on my game. Going into matches with that on my mind was stressful enough, but the other thing which began to play heavily on my emotions at this time was the level of deceit I had got myself into.

I kept things back from Fiona, my family and from friends. I was able to keep up the façade of having money even when I didn't and, believe me, sometimes I really did not have a coin in my pocket. I quite literally would not have had enough money to go down to the shop and buy a loaf of bread, it was that bad. I knew I had money coming in because of my snooker but that didn't mean there weren't huge gaps for me at times where I had spent all the cash I had. I would sometimes go to Barry Hearn and tell him I might need some extra money for something which sounded perfectly innocent. I might say it was to buy furniture or for building work, anything that came to mind and would look like a decent reason for wanting money, but the reality of it was that I needed the dough in order to gamble.

I was telling so many 'white lies' as I liked to think of them, that it was another strain trying to remember what I'd said to different people as I covered up what was really going on. In my own mind I'd actually convinced myself that all I needed was time to sort the whole mess out, and that by telling these lies I would be able to give myself that time.

The number of lies I told was frightening. Most of them were because of my gambling, but during this whole sorry chapter of my life something else had happened which was eventually to cause the break-up of my marriage, as I left Fiona and the children to live with another woman.

As I admitted before, I had been unfaithful to Fiona during our time together, and while she found out about a couple of these affairs, she was big enough to forgive my indiscretions. I don't kid myself that I was the most handsome guy around and a lot of the time it was simply a case of women being seduced by my celebrity rather than by my looks.

There were always women around when we were taking part in tournaments. I suppose you could say these women were 'snooker groupies,' and they were always keen to get close to the players. It could start with a chat after playing a match or they might turn up at your hotel. Having a drink or a meal could quickly lead on to other things, and I'm not proud of the fact that I did succumb to this sort of temptation on occasions during a certain part of my life. It's an easy thing to do, particularly when you are away from home, but that doesn't mean I don't have regrets. The fact of the matter is that I was pretty much free to do what I wanted from quite an early age which gave me a taste for having fun. Girls were part of that fun and I suppose I took full advantage of the fact that being a well-known snooker player made things a lot easier for me. But there was one woman I met who turned out to be more than just a passing fling, and my involvement with her eventually led to me walking out on my wife and kids.

Her name was Denise, and it would be wrong to blame her for what I eventually did. It was my decision, and I will always carry the burden of knowing what it must have done to my kids at the time. Marriage break-ups are never pleasant, and sometimes they can be very nasty and unpleasant, not just for the husband and wife, but perhaps more importantly for the children involved. It's upsetting enough when things are not right between couples, but they are adults and ultimately it is their own problems which they have to deal with. The real losers in all of this are the children. Suddenly their lives change dramatically and they have to come to terms with the fact that their mother and father are no longer living together. Worse still must be the thought that their parents don't like each other anymore. I can only imagine how crushing that must be for children caught up in a break-up and how difficult it must be for them to have to cope with it. The twins and Tahli were too young to rationalise what had gone on; all they knew was that their daddy was no longer living in the house they called home and that if they were going to see him it would be somewhere else and with a woman who wasn't their mother.

Quite often there is a guilty party when a couple splits up, and in my case it was me. I had gone off with another woman, but it was not just a mild flirtation or fling. I had fallen in love with Denise.

We met when I was in Sheffield for the World Championship at the Crucible. There used to be a menswear shop in the city which sold great clothes, and whenever I was there I would always pay a visit and buy a jacket or pair of trousers. It was almost like an annual ritual when I played in the championship. On this particular occasion I walked into the shop and started chatting to a girl who was working there. She turned out to be the sister-in-law of the guy who owned the place. It was one of those meetings which felt comfortable and relaxed, it was as if we'd known each other for a while instead of just having met for the first time. We both found it easy to talk to each other, and for the next two months we basically ended up having an affair on the telephone and fell in love. We were always talking to each other, and the relationship blossomed after that initial meeting in Sheffield. It carried on for about 18 months before Fiona eventually found out and things came to a head.

I left the house and moved in with Denise who had an apartment in Sheffield. At first the kids used to come and visit me, but I think Fiona understandably had a lot of negative thoughts about me and what I had done. They were certainly transmitted to the children and it became a very difficult situation for me to have to deal with.

I am not looking for sympathy because I know I brought the whole thing on myself. I was a coward in the way that

I went about dealing with the situation. I just walked out and turned my back on things, instead of taking full responsibility for my actions and confronting any problems I had head on – a common theme throughout my life and something I am not proud of.

I'd like to think that I have changed and would never act again in the way I did back then. I hope I have learned from some of the dreadful things I have done in the past, but what I cannot do is pretend they didn't happen. I have to accept the consequences of my actions and face up to the mistakes I made, but that doesn't mean I can undo what has already been done. My children suffered because of what I did. I walked out and left them. I wasn't there for them when they needed me, and that hurts. I love them dearly and I know I have caused them all sorts of pain and anguish during their lives. I was not a good father then, and it must have hurt them during that horrible period. They didn't deserve to have to go through what they did and, although I can't alter the past, I hope they now realise just how sorry I am for my actions and how deeply I love all of them. Fiona suffered too, and that must have been terrible for her. In the years which followed she showed just what a brilliant mother she was to our children; she was superb and deserves so much credit after all that happened when I walked out.

That whole sorry period of my life with my gambling escalating out of control, my marriage breaking up and my finances in such a perilous state was an absolute nightmare. Gambling was at the root of so much that had gone wrong, but I was addicted and, no matter what had happened and what might lay in store for me around the corner, I was not about to stop betting.

The nightmare was not about to end and, in fact, worse was yet to come.

CHAPTER ELEVEN

BANKRUPT

There was a huge stigma attached to bankruptcy in my mind. Perhaps it was a generational thing. I grew up in an era when going bankrupt conjured up all sorts of images of someone who had failed in life, who had done something wrong, who had people talking about them behind their backs, and who was some sort of social outcast. There was no way on earth I ever wanted to join the list of people who had been declared bankrupt, but what I didn't realise during the early part of the 1990s was that my awful financial state was leading me towards that very course of action.

After almost seven years with Barry Hearn and Matchroom I left the organisation. There were no arguments or bad feelings on either side, the relationship had just run its course. Barry was getting more involved in the boxing promotion side of his business, and the best years of my snooker career were behind me, even though I would never have admitted it at the time. I have nothing but good things to say about Barry – he was good for my career and I like to think I was good for him and Matchroom during the time I was with them. I have great memories of my time as part of the set-up, and also of the laughs and friendships I had with the rest of the lads. My problem gambling really kicked in during my last couple of years with Barry, but he was unaware of it. When I left I still thought things would be fine and that I would branch out on my own and continue my snooker career.

I was well established as a player and with the public, but snooker's popularity had probably already peaked in this country during the Eighties. As the new decade dawned, things weren't quite the same, but the sport had become more established and several tournaments were now part of the regular scheduling for the various television channels. I was still good enough to earn pretty decent money and, although the exhibition circuit wasn't quite as lucrative as it had been, there was still work to be had. I thought I would be alright without being part of Matchroom. I could get work and wouldn't be paying Barry his 20 per cent anymore, so that should have been a help as well when it came to my overall earning capacity, but the real problem for me was the fact that gambling had eroded away so much of what I had earned in the past.

About six or eight months after leaving Barry, my accountant let me know the full extent of the mess I had got myself into. I owed money but didn't have enough to settle everything I needed to. My house in Great Glen might have helped to stave all of this off if I had been able to sell it for the price I wanted. It went on the market for £450,000 and there was a buyer for it the next day who was willing to pay £400,000 for it, but the sale never happened, and by the time the was eventually sold it, there had been a property crash and it went for about £280,000, which was a huge difference. That difference might just have been enough to keep my head above water, but I lost out on getting near to the full price and I also lost out in my gambling. In 1992 I was declared bankrupt. It was not a pleasant experience, but in a strange kind of way I saw it as the opportunity to make a fresh start for myself.

Being bankrupt meant I didn't have things like credit cards or bank accounts, and in a strange way that gave me a degree of freedom. The break from Fiona had not been pleasant, and the aftermath of it was equally nasty because the story was splashed all across a Sunday newspaper, with me cast as the love rat who had walked out on his wife and kids to live with his mistress. It wasn't nice for me, but equally it must have been horrible for my children and Fiona, not to mention Denise who got a real taste of what it could be like if you are associated with someone in the public eye.

I have always thought that to a large extent my fame has worked in my favour over the years, and certainly there has been more good publicity than bad. I have enjoyed the rewards of that and have been grateful for it, but when you are on the wrong end of a story, as I had been in Sheffield during the 1982 World Championship, it is not a pleasant experience. It's one thing beaming for a camera when you've won a tournament or been involved in a great game of snooker, but it's a different matter when you feel that the eyes of the world are on you, passing judgement on something you are not particularly proud of and which is a very personal matter. Press photographers would stand on my doorstep ready to take pictures whenever I went out into the street, and the fact that I was also in a bad way financially made it even worse. There was nothing I could do except ride out the storm. Ultimately, you are not news for long, the novelty wears off and some other poor soul comes along who they find more interesting, as their private life is raked over in public. It's just the way things are, and I accept that as a public figure it's all part of the game.

The amazing thing is that throughout all of the problems, both financial and marital, I was immersed in before I went bankrupt, it still didn't stop me from betting. It was as if I had a complete blind spot to what was the obvious common thread for so much that had gone wrong. I carried on trying to win money, and the fact that I was still a 'name' and a 'face' in the racing world allowed me to keep gambling. I admit to having an ego, and I actually liked the fact that some of the punters at racecourses would be intrigued to see who I was having a bet on when I was at a track. I was able to use my web of accounts to keep going, betting money that I couldn't afford to lose, but sometimes also betting money that wasn't even mine.

You don't spend a lifetime in the world of betting and gambling as I had without coming across some people who are not exactly whiter than white. I have already talked about the betting culture in the old billiard hall days and the shady characters the places attracted. It's fair to say that over the years I have mixed with and met some people who might not have earned their money in the most orthodox way. That was just part of the world I inhabited.

Through various contacts I was once introduced to somebody who might well have had underworld connections. I honestly don't know for sure, because it's not the sort of thing you ask. I was told this guy had very good contacts in the racing world and when it came to getting information about horses and how they might perform, he knew his stuff. He knew 'exactly the time of day', as they say, meaning that he knew everything that was going on and the people who were involved. His contacts were that good. The one drawback for him was that he wasn't able to place the sort of hefty bets he wanted to with all the various bookies. I, on the other hand, had no such problems, and so I agreed to front some bets for him. He would tell me the money he wanted to lay and I would usually put some dough on myself, because his information was so good.

The arrangement worked well and we had some good bets and others which didn't quite come off, but on one particular occasion it all went very badly wrong for me. He knew I could put some big sums on with the bookies and would phone me up to say what he wanted to bet on. He'd ask me to maybe put £40,000 on one particular horse and then another time he'd ring and ask me to put £20,000 on another. It wasn't every day and it was only when he thought he'd got enough good information to make it worthwhile putting a big bet on. Nobody questioned the amounts I put on because they weren't out of the ordinary for me, and I was seen as someone who could back up any wager I placed, otherwise I would never have been allowed the accounts I had with all the various bookmakers.

I'd had a decent win with some bookies, one of whom

was Victor Chandler, but on my next excursion to a course I'd placed some big bets and lost the money. The thing was that the guy who I had been laying the bets for suddenly told me he didn't have the money to pay off the debt. He wasn't the sort of person I was going to have an argument with, and it was a genuine thing anyway. He wasn't trying to bump me for the money, he simply didn't have it. He might have been doing the same size of bets with about 20 other people as he was with me, and if that was the case then a losing bet could have cost him hundreds of thousands of pounds. The situation might have changed three or six months down the line, but I wasn't about to get that sort of time to pay. Not unreasonably, Victor wanted the money I owed him. I'd had a good win off him a few weeks earlier, and he obviously thought all the money I'd won was mine and that I should be able pay. I might have kept some from the amount I'd put on myself, but the rest belonged to the guy I had laid the bet for. I asked for some time to pay but he wasn't having it, and neither was another little bookmaking firm from Brighton. Instead they got me 'warned off'. Put in layman's terms it meant that I was no longer allowed to go to any racetrack in the country. A bet is a debt of honour, and I had not been able to pay the debt I owed. Victor was quite within his rights to do what he did, but it was a shame our relationship ended in the way it did. I liked Victor a lot, and he took me racing to places like Paris during the time we knew each other. When it happened I might for a fleeting moment have thought it could be a blessing in disguise, because at least it meant I wouldn't be able to visit a race-track again and I could concentrate on my snooker, but any such thought was extremely brief because I did what any gambler would have done and immediately started using betting shops. And so I continued on my self-destructive path.

I had been dicing with gambling death for long enough, and it had finally all caught up with me. I'd been in all sorts of holes before but managed to somehow pull myself out of them. I remember going to Ascot one day needing to come out a winner because of the trouble I was in. I had backed a horse over a period of time, putting on different bets which would have ended up winning me the best part of £100,000. As usual I had only backed it because I'd been given good information which said that the horse would do really well and should win. If there is one thing which is a certainty, it is that saying a horse should win a race is very different to it actually doing so. The horse I backed that day should have won the race, in fact it came very close to finishing ahead of the field, but not close enough – it was beaten by a short head.

I remember leaving the course that day and thinking that I was 'gone.' By that I mean that financially I had been wiped out. It seemed impossible for me to get out of the mess, but somehow I did, putting some gambling wins together which were enough to give me more breathing space, but it hadn't stopped there. I continued to bet until right up to the moment bankruptcy became inevitable. There were only so many times I could keep going to the well. In the end there was a realisation that I wasn't going to be able to get myself out of the mess I was in, and being bankrupt at least gave me the chance to start again and rebuild my life. Or at least it should have.

For a time I think that's what it did. In my own mind I suppose I thought the slate had been wiped clean, I could move on and start to think about the future. All of this might have worked had it not been for one thing: my compulsion to gamble.

The way in which I could bet may have changed, but it didn't stop me doing something that had been second nature to the way I went about my life for so long. If there was anything good which came out of me becoming bankrupt, perhaps it was the fact that it slowed me down a little, but that didn't really last too long.

After I became bankrupt, I felt I was more controlled in the way that I went about my betting compared to the way I had been before, but to most people it would have seemed as though I was still behaving like an idiot. My idea of 'control' was to bet a couple of thousand instead of the £10,000 or £20,000 I might have tried to do before. I still had good contacts in the horse racing world and so the tips and information I always liked to have before placing a bet was there for me and I used them. I also had my own knowledge of snooker and who might be good bets in different tournaments.

I had settled down to life with Denise in Sheffield, but because I was still competing on the snooker circuit I was away from home quite a lot of the time. She had her own job and we tended to live quite independent lives, but we also had a really nice time when were together as a couple. She was aware of all that had gone on with me in the past and that I liked to gamble, but I don't think she was aware of the fact that I was still betting as heavily as I was. It was easy not to let her know, because we had a pretty decent lifestyle and somehow I managed to get the bills paid. We got on very well and, despite having jobs which kept us apart for long periods at time, the relationship continued and I think we were both very happy. My gambling pattern may have changed because I no longer went to race tracks, but I could still bet and, despite all the problems I had been through, I continued to have the gambler's mentality of thinking the next bet would be the big win I was looking for. I was always after a better lifestyle than I had, even though the one I did have wasn't awful. I always seemed to be chasing something else and, although I used to think that gambling was a way of giving me what I wanted, the opposite was in fact true.

Going bankrupt was a horrible experience, and it made me feel awful at the time it happened. I couldn't help thinking that people would be talking about me behind my back and making judgements. Whether that happened or not, I don't know, but it was the feeling it gave me which I found very uncomfortable to deal with at first. As time went on I got over those initial feelings and in many ways things began to return to normal. Well, normal for me. Not having credit cards or bank accounts didn't really bother me. I was still able to bet and used cash – my only problem was that I never seemed to have enough of it. Without doubt I was past my best as a snooker player, but I was still a big enough name to be playing regularly and competing at the top of the game. I liked playing the big tournaments, even if the chance of me winning one of them had passed some time before. I'm sure age was catching up with me, but my gambling must also have been a factor in my decline because it brought constant financial worries.

By the time the 1994 World Championship came around, I had just turned 40. Nobody expected me to be a winner in Sheffield, including me, but I enjoyed competing in the tournament, and as well as playing I was also due to get involved in some commentating for the BBC, something I enjoyed doing and which had started some years earlier for me when I worked on *Junior Pot Black*, and commentated on a promising Scottish youngster named Stephen Hendry.

I got through my first-round match beating Gary Ponting 10-2, but then came unstuck against Darren Morgan in the second round, losing 13-12. Apart from my work with the BBC, I was also due to do a bit of work with the championship sponsors, Embassy. They had a hospitality area and I was in there, along with John Virgo and Dennis Taylor, chatting and meeting people when somebody mentioned the fact that one of the girls in another part of the suite was a former Miss Great Britain.

I have to admit that by this time my traveling and general lifestyle of being on the road as a snooker player had probably seen Denise and I grow apart. Not in the sense that we were unhappy with each other or constantly having rows when we were in each other's company, but simply because we really weren't spending that much time together. I was on the snooker circuit and had also got involved in things like celebrity golfing weekends, which once again meant I was away from home a lot of the time. My weakness for female company had not gone away and, although neither of us really knew it at that time, our relationship was coming to an end.

Once I'd heard about this ex-beauty queen working at the championship, I couldn't wait to see what she looked like. Sure enough, when I did get to meet her she was a real stunner, a beautiful girl with a wonderful personality. If there is such a thing as love at first sight, then it probably happened to me that night. I chatted to her and joked around before suggesting that we had dinner.

Her name was Jill Saxby and she had won her Miss Great Britain title nine years earlier. She had only been working at the championship that day because a friend of hers had been taken ill and she had stepped in and taken her place. During the course of our meal that evening she told me that she had recently left her husband. I felt as though it was fate meeting her when I did, and it didn't take me long to realise I was well and truly taken with her. I saw a lot of her during the course of the championship and realised long before the end that I had fallen in love with her. It wasn't just the way she looked, it was much deeper than that. She was wonderful to talk to and we got on so well. There were the usual laughs and jokes to begin with, but I think both of us understood that we were not just going to have a brief encounter and then move on. This was something very different, something that was going to be special.

Jill lived just outside of Sheffield, and we continued to meet after the World Championship. We had to be discreet because Sheffield and its surrounding area is not a huge place and I think both of us realised that it probably wouldn't be long before Denise found out about the two of us. It wasn't a comfortable situation for me, but, once again, I took the easy way out by not owning up to Denise and telling her that I was in love with another woman. The nature of my job allowed me to put the moment off because I was not at the apartment too often and Denise's work also kept her busy, but there was still no excuse. I let it drift and continued seeing Jill.

It was always going to be the case that Denise would find out about us, one way or another, and that happened one day some weeks later when somebody told her what had been going on. It couldn't have been nice for her to hear it from a third party rather than from me, but once the secret was out both of us had to deal with it. She was obviously hurt and upset by my deceit, and she wanted to know whether I was going to stop seeing Jill and stay with her, or leave.

I really cared a lot for Denise, even at that point in our relationship, but I'd met someone I was very much in love with. What might have started as a bit of curiosity with me wanting to see what former a Miss Great Britain winner looked like had very quickly developed into something much more meaningful and important to the two of us. It might have taken me a while, but I knew that at last I had found the perfect woman for me.

CHAPTER TWELVE

SICK AS A PARROTT

Having made the decision to split up with Denise and move out of her apartment, I found myself without a permanent home of my own. Jill was living in rented accommodation with her two young children in Stocksbridge near Sheffield, and I needed a base of my own as I tried to get on with my life, so I decided to move back to the familiar territory of Leicester to a little place just outside the city called Thornton. At the time my mum lived there, and I moved in with her. It was good for me to have a base, and I think my mother was happy to have me there with her while Jill and I decided what we were going to do.

For quite a few months I would travel up to see her or she would pop down, but it certainly wasn't an ideal situation and we both knew that we wanted to settle down together at some stage and have a place of our own. I knew that Jill was right for me, but I also knew that I came with a lot of baggage. Before we met and got to know each other the only view she would have had of me would have been the one I regularly presented to the public. But once it was obvious that we were on our way to having a serious relationship there was no way I could try to hide what had already gone on in my life.

Jill soon came to realise that I was no angel and that I had let my love of gambling get me into all sorts of problems, culminating in my bankruptcy a little more than two years before we met. I might have had a career as a high-profile snooker player, but she soon realised that I had not looked after my money and there was certainly no millionaire lifestyle awaiting her. In many ways it was quite the opposite because unlike a lot of other people I didn't have a guaranteed income. I wasn't on a salary which gave me regular money each month. Everything I earned was variable, and there could be good and bad months. I was able to look at my diary, see what was booked in there and know what I was going to be getting in the weeks and months ahead, but when it came to things like tournaments the income from them would completely depend on how successful I was. I still did exhibitions as well and had started to do bits of commentary for the various television companies. Although I was past my snooker best, I could still compete and, luckily for me, my distinctive appearance also seemed to help when getting some extra work. I had always been able to duck and dive in order to get money, and I was doing more and more of it at this stage in my life.

None of this was hidden from Jill. I was very up-front about my chequered past, and she also knew about the break-up of my marriage. My wandering ways with the ladies while I was still in a relationship is not something I am proud of as I look back on my life. It couldn't have been nice for Fiona or Denise to find out what had been going on behind their backs; it was not something I ever planned or set out to do, it just happened. But that side of my life became a thing of the past once I had met Jill, and in the years which have followed she has been the only woman for me. Jill is a very special person, and even in those very early months after we first met I think we both felt that we had a special kind of relationship, although I'm equally sure now that neither of us could have thought it would go on to be tested in quite the way that it was. I knew I was lucky to have found her then, and that feeling has only strengthened in the years since.

Although Jill knew about my gambling, she wasn't aware of the full extent of my compulsion. This wasn't because I deliberately set out to keep things back from her, it was just a case of me carrying on in the way I always had done. As far as I was concerned, I liked to bet – I didn't have a gambling problem. From time to time things might get a little bit tough financially, but I always felt I was capable of sorting those problems out. It's the kind of delusion any addicted gambler will employ to justify what they do, and in a strange way it also gave me a clear conscience because I convinced myself that ultimately things were under control.

I know people will wonder how I could possibly believe I was building an honest and open relationship with a woman I loved, if I kept the full extent of my gambling from her. The honest answer is that, because of my mindset as someone who had done this sort of thing since he was a teenager, I saw nothing wrong with it. I didn't feel I was being dishonest, I was just getting on with my life and trying to make some money for the two of us. Gambling had long since stopped being just a hobby for me – although that is probably what I would have called it had I been asked – but the reality was that it had acted as a twin career for longer than I cared to remember. I wasn't a professional gambler, but I was very much a regular one, and over the years I had thrown thousands and thousands of pounds at trying to make sure I stayed ahead of the game and made money from my betting. The fact that gambling had caused all sorts of problems didn't deter me at all. Amazing as it may sound, it probably made me all the more determined to carry on because, like all gamblers, I was convinced that by betting more and more I would eventually come out on top.

Just a couple of years after bankruptcy, it was pretty much business as usual for me. I had nothing like the sort of accounts or access to credit I'd had in the past, so I wasn't able to bet some of the vast sums I had before (I know now that if I could have done, I would). Instead I had to content myself with laying relatively modest bets of £2,000 and £3,000. Again I became quite adept at being able to shift money around from the few accounts I did have in order to keep them open and functioning for me. Slowly but surely I began to get myself in trouble again because of my gambling, and once more I found myself feeling stressed and depressed at the situation I found myself in.

Jill and I had managed to find a house in Leicestershire that we both liked, and it was going to cost £175,000. The repayments on the mortgage were going to be around £800 a month and I was also paying alimony to Fiona. It meant that with the mortgage and the alimony I was going to have to find about £2,000 every month to cover the cost, and that was before any of the other domestic bills had to be taken care of.

By 1996, I had slipped further down the snooker ladder to number 25 in the rankings and that meant a reduction in my earning power. Only the top 16 players qualified automatically for the final stages of major tournaments, thus guaranteeing them reasonable money, while players ranked from 17-32 had to play a pre-qualifying match to get there. This could often mean having to play against some very good younger players, such as Ronnie O'Sullivan, John Higgins and Paul Hunter, who were coming through at the time. This meant it became harder and harder to progress in tournaments and inevitably this led to a reduction in things like personal appearances and invitational events. In 1995, I'd played in one such event, the Regal Scottish Masters, which was staged at the Civic Centre in Motherwell. In 1996, I was not invited back. It was the sort of thing that was happening more and more.

At the age of 42 I was well and truly into the twilight of my snooker career. The thing which I had always felt would go on forever was now showing distinct signs of drawing to a close. I knew it was happening but didn't really want to admit it to myself or anyone else. I felt that by carrying on in the way I always had done I would be able to stay on the circuit, and if the odd tournament dried up and I wasn't going to be part of it I would have to find other ways of making up the shortfall.

I enjoyed commentating on tournaments for television and was always keen to learn more about the craft whenever I worked in the commentary box. In the past I had played in events and then got involved on the television side of things whenever I'd been knocked out. It worked well, and I was gaining experience all the time working behind the microphone. I suppose that at the back of my mind I also saw it as a new avenue of income for me. Even though the money wasn't huge, it still came in useful. Although I hadn't been invited to play in the Scottish Masters by the organisers that year, I had been asked to do some television work by BBC Scotland, so I was going to be involved in the tournament, even if it was as an outsider, watching my fellow professionals compete for the title.

By the time the Masters came around my finances were once again in a complete mess. I owed money on my betting accounts and I owed money to individuals I had borrowed from. I was trying once more to keep my head above water and was not doing a very good job of it.

Jill and I had just moved into our new house, and I was so desperate for the whole thing to work out between us. We had her two children, Natalie who was eight years old and James, five, living with us and it felt like we were a family. I now had a home which I hoped my own children would be able to visit and enjoy as well, and, happily, that was something which did later happen. However, as I drove up to Motherwell to fulfil my BBC commitments I was at one of my lowest points. I was deeply in debt with various accounts due to be paid in a matter of days. Jill was unaware of how much trouble I was in because I'd kept it from her, partly because I still believed that somehow I would find a way out of my predicament and partly because I certainly didn't want her to have to worry about where the next pound was coming from. It was still only a couple of years since we'd first met and I didn't want to screw up our relationship by letting her know how bad things were, but as I sat in my car during the four-hour journey up to Scotland my thoughts kept drifting back to money and the trouble I was in.

It had been no better when I was at home. I would lie awake at night going over everything in my mind, before making an excuse to Jill and wandering downstairs to sit on my own in front of the television. I was depressed about my finances, my career as a snooker player and about what the future might hold for me. I was also depressed about the fact that I had weaved a web of deceit. I had borrowed money from people, from family, friends and various contacts in the gambling world, and not told them the full extent of my problems or the reason for borrowing the money. As far as they were concerned, I was just short of a few bob and they were helping me out with loans which I would pay back when I got myself straight. It meant my finances became even more complicated as I tried to juggle things around to make sure people were paid when I promised they would be. Sometimes I would borrow money and honestly believe at the time I did it that I would only need it for a few days to see me through a difficult patch, but then I would use it to have a bet on a horse that didn't win and I would have to go back and make my excuses, asking for more time to repay the cash.

When I travelled to Scotland I probably had about £300 in my pocket, but it was pretty much all the cash I could lay my hands on. I was feeling pretty awful, and the solitude did nothing to lift my gloom; instead it just allowed me more time to realise just what a mess I was in. By the time I reached my hotel it felt as if my life was about to fall apart again. Having gone through the whole bankruptcy thing once, I certainly didn't want to go through all that again, but I could only see things getting worse unless I could reverse the trend by getting a much needed cash injection.

My debts amounted to around £20,000 at this time. Not as high as they had been in the past, but now that my prospects of big snooker paydays had diminished these debts were devastating.

Luckily, when I arrived, my old mate Dennis Taylor was staying at the same hotel and at least I was able to have a bit of a laugh with him. It raised my spirits and also meant that for a while at least I was able to escape from all the doom and gloom which had occupied my thoughts during the drive up in my car. Dennis suggested that we go out for a meal, something we had always done together during our touring days with Matchrooom, and we decided to visit a Chinese restaurant we'd been to the year before when I'd played in the tournament. While we were in there John Parrott came in to get a takeaway. John was another player I had always got on well with, and we always seemed to have a giggle when we were together. I really liked his sense of humour and I expected him to come out with a remark that would have all of us laughing just as he had done so often in the past, but when I saw his face I could see that he was not in a joking mood.

"I've only had my cue nicked," he told us.

John explained that his car had been broken into at Heathrow airport. He had a new cue for the tournament but, as I have explained, for a serious player a snooker cue is like an extension of their arm. Poor John knew his game was going to be badly affected by what had happened, and he wasn't looking forward to having to play with his new cue.

"I'm playing awful with it – you know what it's like, it just doesn't feel right," he confided. "Willie, do yourself a favour," he added. "Don't back me tomorrow!"

Just like anyone else on the circuit, John was well aware that I liked a bet, but I think he said it more as a throwaway line, trying to make a joke out of a bad situation. But even as he said it my mind had started buzzing with the possibility of turning this whole situation to my advantage. Poor old John might have lost his cue, but every cloud has a silver lining and I quickly began to realise what that could be. The silver lining I was thinking about might not have been of any use to him, but I knew it could be an absolute lifesaver for me. As far as I was concerned, there was no way on earth John was now going to be able to beat his opponent, Ken Doherty, who he was due to meet the next day. The handicap of having to play with a new cue was going to be too much to cope with, leaving only one possible outcome: a win for Ken.

It was so obvious that it was almost too good to be true. It was like having another Isle of Wight moment. Obviously, it wasn't quite the same because John's match with Doherty hadn't actually been played, but I saw it as the next best thing because I just couldn't see John being able to win.

My mind went into overdrive while I was still sitting at the table with Dennis and it wasn't long before I was trying to convince him and as many friends and contacts as I could that I was putting them onto a sure thing. I was convinced that John would lose to Ken the next day, so they all needed to get some money on the result. When I got back to my hotel I immediately started to ring round all the people I thought could be of use. The betting had to be made in relatively small amounts so that it did not alert anyone to the fact that there might be something going on. I managed to get some credit with people like Racing Raymond in order to put around £5,000 on Doherty, because he immediately realised I was on to something after I'd explained what had happened. I did the same with several other contacts, as well as phoning up friends to tell them the same story so that they could get in on the action and earn a nice bit of easy money for themselves. I'd managed to convince Dennis as well, and he'd phoned his son up to make sure he had a bet on the outcome as well. By the time I had finished making my calls it was late, but I was sure it was all going to be worthwhile.

I still had more calls to make early on in the morning before the various bookmakers opened. I was asking people to put £1,000 or £1,500 for me and then the same or a bit more for themselves. The bets weren't large in themselves but by the time I'd finished I worked out that I'd put about £38,000 on a win for Doherty, it might even have been a little bit more. I'd exhausted every avenue I knew in a bid to make sure I made the most of what I considered to be a sure thing. The amount that had been put on a Doherty win did eventually cause the betting to be suspended later that morning, but by that time I could content myself with the knowledge that all I really had to do was sit back and wait for the money to roll in. I had done nothing wrong, nothing illegal. I had just used the system and now I was about to beat it.

I always like the atmosphere you get at a tournament, but as I made my way to the commentary box after lunch that day I felt better than I had done for months. All the days and weeks of worrying about where the next pound was going to come from would soon be sorted out thanks to a bit of good fortune. I reasoned that I deserved a bit of luck for once after all I had gone through recently. It was my turn to get my own back and I was about to do it in spectacular fashion.

I settled down in the box and began to look forward to the match. It was best of 11 frames, and I had more than the usual anticipation as John and Ken made their way to the table. The odds I'd managed to get weren't massive but they were good enough for me to expect to make more than £30,000, which was enough to wipe away all my money problems.

The match started in the fashion I expected, with John not looking particularly comfortable with his new cue, and as a consequence he didn't really offer too much resistance as Ken took the first frame. I couldn't help feeling a tinge of excitement as the frame ended, but at the same time I also knew that I had a job to do and, although I might have been talking a bit more than I should because of what was happening, I managed to keep myself under control and instead offered sympathy to John, telling the television audience how tough it had to be for him following the loss of his regular cue. The second frame seemed to highlight just how tough it was for John as he made some bad mistakes, allowing Ken to make a break of 70 and win it.

It all seemed to be going the way I had thought it would with Ken looking comfortable and in control of the match, but somehow or other without looking at all convincing John began to claw his way back into the game. He made some 20 breaks and chipped away at Ken to take the next two frames and level the match. I was amazed that he'd been able to do what he did, because the two frames had come out of nothing. It wasn't as if John had suddenly rediscovered his form; he still looked out of sorts, but at the same time he'd managed to hang in there and fight his way back to make it all square at the interval.

I may have been surprised at what had happened, but I was still confident that the outcome would see me getting the money that would go some way to easing my finances, and in typical gambler's fashion I was also looking forward to having a bit of cash to use for further betting, which I believed would bring in even more money. I was still daydreaming during the break in proceedings when I bumped into John who was bemoaning his form and told me he just wasn't able to get anything going with the cue he was using. It was a shame for him, but at the same time it was music to my ears. Despite the fact that he'd managed

SICK AS A PARROTT

to pull himself level, he was obviously uncomfortable with his game and, when he told me that, I felt my money was safe.

What happened when the match resumed soon shook me out of my complacency. He might still have looked awkward but John managed to continue where he had left off before the break and somehow scrambled his way to a third consecutive frame. His snooker still looked poor with no great consistency, but worse was to come for me as he grabbed another two frames to make the score 5-2, he just one frame from victory.

I couldn't believe what was happening and the confidence I'd had in the outcome of the result began to drain away. To make matters even more difficult for me I had to commentate on the whole thing live. I knew I had to continue doing a professional job, and I believe I did just that, but at the same time my masterplan was going disastrously wrong. I might not have been physically sweating, but my stress levels must have been sky high, and my stomach was churning as the eighth frame began. When Ken clinched it I began to breathe a little easier – surely it would now signal a change in the way the game had gone, with Ken coming from behind to take the match. John hadn't even put together a 50 break during the course of winning his five frames, and he didn't make one in the next frame either, but still did enough to win it, and the match.

I could feel the blood drain from my face as I sat in the box and went into a kind of auto-pilot mode. I was talking as if it was just another match and explained to those watching their television screens that without ever having played well, and with a completely new cue, John Parrott had somehow managed to snatch victory in a match he had looked like losing. It was a remarkable win and I told the watching millions just that, but as the words came out of my mouth my mind was spinning. I had just seen what the impossible happen before my very eyes.

Nobody at the venue, with the exception of Dennis, knew I had been betting on a Ken win, but even he didn't know the extent to which I had bet or how important winning the money was to me. I had missed out on a windfall by placing bets on Ken, and that was bad enough, but in doing so I had also convinced a lot of other people to put money on him as well. It was a horrible feeling as I put the microphone and headphones down after finishing my commentating stint.

I can't honestly remember if I talked to anyone on the way out of the Civic Centre, but I do remember getting into my car for the short drive to my hotel. When I got there I went straight to my room and sat on the end of my bed with my head in my hands.

The gambling instinct within me had seen me make another decision in my life which had gone badly wrong. Things had been bad enough before I got to Motherwell, and for a fleeting few hours I thought my luck was finally going to change, but I should have known better. You can't carry on betting unless there is an optimistic streak within your personality. Whatever goes wrong, the gambling instinct drives you on to believe that just around the corner there is another opportunity that will make up for any disappointment you may have experienced.

What John had done seemed impossible to me, not getting one single 50 break and yet still managing to come back from being two frames behind. When I look back on my life now and at all the different bets I've had over the years I can clearly see that I was not one of life's lucky gamblers. I was never one of those people who always seemed to have bets that worked out for them no matter what. The opposite always seemed true of me. Sure, I had some memorable wins, but there were so many times when the great gambling god was clearly trying to tell me something and I closed my ears to what was being said, refusing to take in what now seems to be so obvious. Getting kicked in the teeth by what had happened in the match between John and Ken should have been more than enough of a warning to me that lady luck wasn't on my side, but my problems were now bigger than ever and in order to solve them I chose a very familiar route.

There was a race meeting going on in Scotland that same week, and I had been given enough good information to make me want to lay some bets that could see me picking up a very decent amount of money. Using my usual network of contacts, I backed three horses, placing £150 each way doubles, and then did £250 each way trebles with the same horses. Things looked good as the first two horses won, and all I needed to pick up around £70,000 was for the third to come in. When the horse came into the home straight about 15 lengths in front and cleared the last fence it looked as though I was home and dry. Nothing could stop it now I thought, and I was right, nothing did as it sailed past the winning post.

The only problem was that about ten yards from the line its saddle cloth came loose and fell to the ground. Without it, the horse, which was called Statajack, couldn't weigh in properly after the race. It's a compulsory part of a racehorse's equipment and as such it meant that Statajack was disqualified after the clerk to the scales objected, saying it had not weighed in as it had gone out. That sort of thing is something that hardly ever happens, but it happened to me. It was unbelievable, and once again I couldn't believe my bad luck. Twice in the space of days I should have been able to make a lot of money and twice I had fallen flat on my face.

On top of all of this I was still doing daily commentating for the BBC, trying to make sure that my chaotic private life did not interfere with what I was supposed to be doing for television. At least I managed to get it right on that front and nobody would have guessed that I'd had such a traumatic time of it with my gambling. In a way I suppose it helped to have something like that to take my mind off what had happened. If I'd been on my own with nothing to occupy my thoughts it would have been a lot worse, but as usual the night time wasn't easy. That was when I had a lot of time on my own to contemplate what was happening and it gave me no comfort at all. And when I spoke to Jill on the telephone, I had to put on a front as if everything was fine.

Towards the end of that week I remember sitting alone in my car and crying as all the emotion of what had happened came pouring out. I desperately wanted things to start to change for me. I'd been given two very harsh lessons in the pitfalls of gambling, but despite what had happened

204

I knew deep down that it wasn't going to stop me having another go. It was what I had done pretty much all of my adult life and I wasn't smart enough to stop.

I had been in bad situations before and got out of them. In one week, my debts had climbed to around £60,000 and yet I still thought that with a change of luck things could improve. Although my career might have been on the slide, I still knew that I could earn a living from being 'Willie Thorne, the snooker player'. I also had enough experience of being able to duck and dive in order to earn some money. There was nothing else I could do except try to carry on in the hope things would eventually turn around for me. I didn't have a clear idea about which direction my life was going to take, but I was finding it harder and harder to be optimistic about what might lie in store for me.

CHAPTER THIRTEEN
THE FINAL STRAW

When I got back from Scotland I knew that my luck would have to change if I was going to keep my head above water financially. I'd had some terrible results with my betting, but that hadn't deterred me from trying to gamble my way out of trouble and amazing as it may sound after all that had already happened to me, I did start to have some successes during the late Nineties. The wins were not enough to lift me out of the mess I was getting into, but I was able to do my usual trick of moving any available cash around in order to stay afloat.

I wasn't only surviving on gambling, I also worked as hard as I could – not just playing snooker, but also doing more things away from the table that brought in some money. I hosted golf days and dinners and continued to work with sponsors and at corporate events, and I would go into a room as if I didn't have a care in the world. I suppose I presented the Willie Thorne they wanted to see, and it probably did me a lot of good too. It was nice to be able to forget my troubles for a few hours and immerse myself in something else. Nobody would have guessed how bad things were for me. It was nice to be able to mix with people, have a chat, tell a few jokes and see that I was making them happy. It gives you a kick when you can walk away from having a chat and can see the person you've been talking to is genuinely pleased that they have met you.

I have always been a grafter. Yes, I liked the idea of making some easy money through betting, but I have never lost sight of the fact that I also needed to work as well. It may seem strange, because I was so undisciplined and chaotic in the way I went about much of my life, but for as long as I can remember a diary has always been a big part of the way I function. I had to plan ahead, and there were always dates and engagements marked off, so despite all of the betting I was never the sort of person who would miss an appointment because of it. I could always organise myself when it involved a snooker tournament, commentating for television or making personal appearances – that side of my life has always been very ordered and precise. But when it came to looking after my finances my approach wasn't quite the same.

I was clearly in a lot of trouble, and it only seemed to be getting worse, no matter how hard I tried to reverse the trend. In many ways I suppose I did have some method to the madness my gambling helped create because I had to keep moving what money I had around. I became very good at making sure I kept some accounts open to bet with and I also tried as best I could to pay people back on time if they loaned me money.

One of the people I went to for money was my own mother. She had always been there for me and, although I might have been able to hide my true emotions from the public, there was no hiding place from my mum. She could see things weren't right with me, and I couldn't pretend otherwise. What I did hide was the full extent of my problems. Borrowing a few thousand pounds from her and then paying it back when I could was very different from telling her the amount I really needed if I was going to get myself out of trouble. It would probably have given her a heart attack. I know she was more than happy to help me out, but I never told her the truth. I lied to my own mother. It is not something I am proud of, and it's just one of a whole list of things I am sorry about and have to try to live with, knowing I can never change what I did.

One of the good things about my life at this time was my relationship with Jill. We enjoyed being together and it was nice to be able to set up home with her, along with young Natalie and James. They were good kids, and one of the lovely things that happened was that my own children would also come over to the house. The children mixed and played together, and everyone got on well, giving the house a happy feel.

These bright times were in stark contrast to some of the lonely nights I began to spend sitting downstairs mulling over my money problems, which seemed to be mounting by the day. In many ways I don't know how I got away with things for so long. I suppose that because every so often there was a cash injection either through snooker and the various offshoots my career had given me, or because

I actually had a decent gambling win now and then, I was able to keep things on a relatively even keel at home. I know that at times I must have been quite difficult to deal with, but Jill always tried to be understanding and supportive if I was in one of my moods. I could snap at her sometimes for no apparent reason, and the fact that money was really tight on occasions didn't help the way I felt.

Jill never demanded money for expensive clothes or luxury items. Obviously, if I had money I happily spent it on her and the kids, but there were other times when I would ask the children why they needed money for some sweets or a can of drink. They were hardly being extravagant and all they were doing was acting like any other children, but if they caught me at a time when I knew there was no real money to speak of and I wasn't too sure where more cash was going to come from, I would give them the whole 20 questions bit. The stupid thing was I was only in the situation of having to worry about money because I'd probably gone out and blown a load of dough on another stupid bet the day before. Again, this will sound like madness to any sane person, but it's familiar territory for any gambling addict.

As the new millennium approached I really didn't have too much to look forward to. I was up to my eyes in debt, my snooker career was coming to an end, I was lying and being deceitful to so many people and I couldn't see a way out of what was becoming a nightmare situation for me. I loved Jill, but at the same time I knew the way I sometimes acted and what was going on financially was bound to start putting a strain on our relationship. I still had the gambler's mindset, thinking something would turn up and that there was surely going to be some way of making money just around the corner, but in reality I was going nowhere fast.

My decline as a player really became apparent during 1994/95 season when my ranking dropped from 15 to 25, but I think it is part of a competitive sportsman's makeup not to face up to reality. Nobody wants to admit that a career is coming to an end, and I was no different in that respect. I kept promising myself that I wasn't that bad and that, although I might not be as good as I once was, I could still cope with the game and had enough natural ability to see me through. The truth was that the shots were becoming harder for me.

Your body naturally changes as you get older. You are not as agile as you once were, you have aches and pains and your hand-to-eye coordination suffers. All this is part of the ageing process for anyone, but when you have to rely on your body and eyes as much as you do when you're a snooker player the problem is more acute. Don't get me wrong, I'm not comparing snooker to something like playing tennis, cricket or football – they are all much more physical and athletic – but you cannot play any sport at the top of the professional tree if your body is in decline. Everything connected with what you do becomes harder, and it doesn't matter if you practise harder or go on various fitness regimes or diets. All of that just staves off the inevitable, and sooner or later you have to own up and call it a day. In my case it was the hand-to-eye coordination which I seemed to have most trouble with. I'd play a shot and think it was going exactly where I wanted it to, but the object ball wouldn't even hit the jaws. When that sort of thing goes it doesn't take long for your confidence to go as well.

The next stage on the way down was when I dropped out of the top 32, at the end of the 1996/97 season, which meant I had to play two qualifying games to reach the final stages of ranking events. Initially, I felt confident about coping with the situation, but any optimism drained away. From a ranking of 35 in 1997, I slipped to 51 and then to 75 by 1999. Often, I'd find myself playing in front of a handful of people in a cubicle at the qualifying venues – so much for being a showman. I wanted to try and maintain my status as a snooker player, but the writing was on the wall. I didn't enjoy having to go through the qualifying process, and once I had dropped out of the top bracket I also found it mentally tough trying to play these matches, knowing how much was riding on them.

Having started playing the game seriously in the 1960s, my snooker career had spanned four decades and several eras in the game. I was a throwback really, because I had come into the professional circuit from the billiard halls, places that were very much part of the scene in the Fifties and Sixties, but which became very old-fashioned and pretty much faded away during the boom years for snooker in the Eighties. As the Nineties drew to a close, I had already slipped too far down the pecking order to think that I could earn decent money from playing and I knew it was time to think about packing the whole thing in. I had to face the fact that I just wasn't good enough anymore.

It was a couple of years before I finally quit, though. By 2001/02, my ranking had fallen so far that I was no longer eligible for the main ranking event circuit and was reduced to competing on the second-tier Challenge Tour. My whole world as a professional player changed. I often found myself playing in clubs where the pockets on the tables could be like buckets, a leveling factor which made it very difficult to beat even an average player. It was a far cry from the heady days of the previous decade, the five-star hotels, the first-class travel, and I found it all quite depressing.

Effectively, my playing career was over long before, but my final match came in 'Challenge Tour: Event 4' at Jesters Snooker Club, Swindon, in early 2002, just before my attempted suicide. I lost 5-1 in the round of the last 32 to Shailesh 'Joe' Jogia, a Leicester lad who'd learnt his trade playing at my snooker centre. My prize money? £250.

As my career petered out I did, however, enjoy one last tournament victory, winning the inaugural World Seniors Masters tournament in 2000 at the age of 46. It was quite a grand affair with each round played over a single frame at the RAC Club in London. It was televised on Sky, and it must have cost a fortune to put together. On the way to the final I beat Joe Johnson, David Taylor and Rex Williams before coming up against my old mate, Cliff Thorburn. I took the frame against Cliff 84-8, making a 60 break in the process, to take the £10,000 first prize – small beer compared to the much bigger sums on offer on the circuit, but very useful money for me at the time – and a claret jug supposedly worth £50,000, which is kept at the RAC Club in Pall Mall, London. Overall, the standard of the snooker played was not good, though, and it was no real surprise that the tournament went missing for several years before being revived recently.

It was a very depressing feeling to know that the game I'd loved playing for so long, and which had been such a part of my life, was now beyond me, or at least playing it to the standard required was. After 25 years as a professional, I had to start looking for other avenues of income.

Ending my playing career was always going to be difficult as it would be for any other player or person who has earned their living from playing sport professionally, but I had the added problem of my finances. Just when I needed more money, I knew I was going to be earning less. For someone like me, the only way I could see myself making the sort of money I needed was to gamble. I went back to doing something that had been disastrous for me in the past – I went on the chase. This involved me making all sorts of bets but, perhaps more dangerously, it also meant that I had to get money by various means in order to do so.

To my mind, placing bets was the quickest way to get some money in, but I also realised I was lucky enough to still have a name and face that people recognised, and I needed to make the most of that as well. My experience of hosting events and being part of the corporate world was something I knew I had to use. One of the first people to ever get me involved in this line of work, back in the early Eighties, was an old school friend named John Hayes. He had a sports sales and promotions business at the time, representing the likes of Gordon Banks, England's former World Cup-winning goalkeeper. John asked me if I would like to be part of some of the corporate events he was involved in, and the one which really got me into the whole thing on quite a big scale was a snooker road show in association with British Telecom.

The roadshow started in Scotland and wound its way south, stopping off at various locations along the way. It was a great format, with two big rooms being used – one for a black-tie dinner with entertainment provided by a singer and comedian and the other room would be used for snooker. I was asked to play three frames against someone like Cliff Thorburn, followed by a celebrity match featuring one of the entertainers who had performed that night, and then there would be a draw, the winner of which would come up and play some frames against either Cliff or I. It always went down well with the people who had come along, and from my point of view it was an easy and enjoyable way of earning decent money for one night's work. I also learnt what it took to make events go well and run smoothly, something which was to be of great importance to me in years to come.

John would often invite me along to various events he was organising such as golf days and dinners, but I was surprised that despite being involved in sports management he never once approached me to see if I would be interested in joining his stable. To be honest, I was a bit put out, particularly as at that time I hadn't even signed with Barry Hearn. It was only years later when the subject came up that he told me he'd always assumed I had someone looking after my affairs.

After coming to the conclusion that my snooker career was over, fate played a hand in bringing John and I together again. He was about to host a big conference at Leicester City Football Club's Filbert Street ground. He needed someone who could host the conference during the day and then do the same for a big dinner that was to be held in the evening. Although we hadn't worked together for some time, he'd kept my number and decided to ring me up and ask if I would be interested in doing the job. It was just the sort of thing I wanted to start doing and, from a practical point of view, I needed all the money I could get.

My finances were in a real state, but perhaps more frightening was the fact that it wasn't just bookmakers who wanted money from me, the Inland Revenue had also become interested in my state of affairs, and when I found out just how much I owed them it looked as though there was no possible way back for me. My gambling was bad enough, but I had also let a lot drift when it came to things like tax returns. I suppose I just couldn't bear to confront my financial demons. The trouble was that the more I ignored things the easier it became to just carry on as if the problems weren't there. I just let the bills and arrears build up, until one day even I had to take notice of what was really happening.

After the Filbert Street conference, which went really well, I began to chat to John about what was happening in my life. I had been approached to work with someone else who we both knew and who had said they wanted me to become involved in some sort of sports management project, but nothing had come of it. John was someone I had known for a long time, he was a very successful businessman and also someone I respected. When he casually suggested that perhaps the two of us could work together with him handling my affairs, it was like music to my ears. I was excited about the prospect and he could see I was interested, but I knew I had to come clean about my tax situation if we were ever going to have the sort of business relationship he was talking about.

"There's one thing I think you should know," I told John. "I owe the Inland Revenue £250,000."

It may sound incredible that I could have allowed things to build up in such a way, because this massive bill had not just appeared overnight – it was a result of not doing anything about the debt and accumulating interest for a number of years. I suppose my attitude towards it all was that in some way or other a big win was going to be just around the corner, or that money from my snooker-playing was somehow going to get to solve the problems I had. Stupid, I know, but that was how I lived my life then.

John was clearly shocked, but he'd known me for a long time and perhaps he wasn't that surprised. He knew I was a gambler and he knew I had been declared bankrupt previously. But I think what did surprise him was the speed with which I'd managed to get myself into such financial bother once again. He had sympathy for my predicament but made a very practical assessment of the situation and explained that I might have to go bankrupt again. The thought of this happening was absolutely awful. I still felt the stigma from when it had happened in 1992, and there was no way I wanted to have to deal with it a second time. It might have been an option and John was right to point it out to me, but the idea filled me with horror and the kind of depression and dread I felt unable to cope with.

"If I have go bankrupt again it's the end, John," I told him.

I'm sure he thought I was just reacting to what was devastating news, and that maybe I wasn't seeing the whole picture, because taking that action would give me a clean slate and the chance to start again. But what he really didn't know was that by "the end" I meant just that. It would be the end of the road for me, because I knew I would top myself.

My depression had got worse and worse in the years leading up to the night I had that conversation with John. Of course, he knew nothing about it and probably thought the same as most other people would have, that I was 'good old Willie', the guy who liked to have a laugh and a joke, who would always be cheerful when he turned up for events, and who was always happy to have a chat with the public. All of that was true, but it also masked what was going on in my own mind at that time. I really couldn't see a way out of my troubles, and when I sat quietly on my own thinking how I desperately wanted something more out of my life I began to think I was never going to get it. I knew I had wasted so much of my life, and just when I wanted to be able to sit back and be able to afford all the things I wanted, I was faced with the reality of not only being unable to do that, but also the prospect of going under once again.

The thought of killing myself had been in my head for a while, usually when I was alone and had time to think about the mess I had made of things financially. During the late 1990s I was occasionally asked to appear at different sporting events abroad and one of them was in Bangkok. I was staying in a lovely hotel in a room near the top of the building. I had a great view, and I can remember walking to the windows one day, looking down at the ground far below me and then thinking to myself that if I had enough courage I could jump and kill myself. I was being perfectly serious. It would have been a way out of my problems and it was something I had started to think more and more about, particularly when I was alone with no distractions.

I loved Jill but I felt I was letting her down more and more. When we'd got together she knew that I'd already had my best years as a snooker player and also that I was a gambler, but that didn't matter to her. She accepted an awful lot right from the beginning of our relationship, and in return I was repeating the same old mistakes. I wanted to be able to get myself out of the mess I was in, but the truth was that I just couldn't really see how that was going to happen.

Meeting up with John again gave me a chance to try and sort myself out. I knew that he had my best interests at heart, but the thought of bankruptcy was too much for me to contemplate and he could see how desperate I was to avoid it happening for a second time so he came up with an alternative course of action.

It was decided that a testimonial year would be organised for me, with various events planned that would hopefully bring in the sort of money needed to satisfy the Revenue. Looking back now, I cannot believe how so many people worked so hard on my behalf to get the whole idea off the ground. It was driven by John and his son Matt, together with an organising committee who worked tirelessly to make sure we hit the ground running. We started 2002 with a huge event one night at Filbert Street that was helped by the incredible generosity of people like comedian Jasper Carrott and rock musician Rick Wakeman who came along and gave their time for absolutely no charge at all. It was a marvelous evening, and it gave me a lift to know that the idea of a testimonial year had taken off in such spectacular fashion. It was also quite emotional for me as well because I realised just how many people in the world of sport and show business seemed to care enough to make the effort to support the testimonial.

As low as I often felt during my bleakest moments at this time, I was lifted by the response. There were people working flat out to organise things quickly and efficiently with the aim of keeping the taxman off of my back. That first event took place on the last Saturday in January, and I later found out that I nearly went under before it had even taken place. The Revenue were going to bust me on 1st February, and I would have been declared bankrupt but, only days before, a cheque for £25,000 was sent off to them which was enough to stop any action they were about to take, and a further guarantee was made that they would receive £100,000 in total. This was going to be financed from all the various events and functions which were planned and John did a deal that involved the Revenue getting £10,000 each month until the £100,000 target was reached. Several other events took place in the next few weeks with more planned throughout the year and, naturally, I was pleased that we were on the way to paying off my huge tax debt.

What didn't please me as much was the fact that I hadn't been entirely truthful with John. I had only told John one part of my story. I was still gambling and it was getting me further and further in trouble. My trick of borrowing from various people in order to keep the habit going and to pay off some of the people I owed could only get me so far. Some of the sums I needed were too big to ask friends to lend me, and I began to enter a world that not only led me to become more deceitful to those closest to me, but also brought me into contact with people who were not going to mess about if I didn't come up with the cash I owed them. I asked around my usual contacts in the gambling world and soon came to the conclusion that the only way to get my hands on the sort of cash sums I needed was to start using money lenders. I was warned by several people that it wasn't exactly the best route I could take and that I could end up getting myself in even bigger trouble, but I was desperate.

While all of this was spinning around in the background I was also trying to carry on leading a normal life. My playing career was effectively over, but I was still closely associated with the game thanks to my work for television and I was also earning decent money making personal appearances. I enjoyed things like golf days, and if you got the right mix of people when you played your round it could be particularly enjoyable. At one of the golf days I found myself talking to a guy who appeared to have his finger on the pulse when it came to the share price of a particular company involved in medical technology. He insisted that if I wanted to make a killing on the stock market I should invest in their shares and that there was no way I could lose. Famous last words, but I had always been a sucker for a bit of good information.

"Do yourself a favour," my new friend told me. "But don't tell anybody else."

Was he kidding? The chances of me not telling anyone else were zero. From what he told me and from what I'd heard about him, I thought I was on to a sure thing. I had never played the markets because I really didn't know enough about them and I never saw the point of just taking a real gamble on something like that. But this was different. I had actually been given a tip and it could end up paying off handsomely not only for me but for quite a few people who I thought I could do a good turn for. I made some calls and spread the word hoping that they would put some money in and make something from the tip I'd given them, and that in turn might prompt them into rewarding me for the information. I found it all really exciting; this was like backing a horse that you knew had already romped home.

I'd had similar feelings in the past and not all of them had come off. The memory of bets like John Parrott losing that match against Ken Doherty should have been ringing alarm bells in my head. But all I could think of was what this could mean to me and the people I'd tipped off, some of whom had put £40,000 or £50,000 into an investment on the back of what I had told them. They trusted my information to be right and that it would make them some money. I'd had a lot of disappointments with my gambling and I was still in trouble because of the mess it had landed me in, but at no time did I see this as a gamble. This wasn't

221

like a race where my horse might get beaten by a short head, this was stocks and shares. It was about a company that was going to manufacture a product that would see its value shoot up. All everyone had to do was sit back and wait for it to happen. But instead of soaring to the sky, shares in the company dropped like a stone, and those people I had given the tip to saw the prospect of making a killing disappear overnight.

It was a horrible feeling. I hadn't forced anyone to put their money into the shares, they were all speculating on a tip I'd given them, but at the same time I just felt like I'd let so many people down. I'd tried to do something that would help them out and at the same time do me a favour as well. I had been in a really depressed state when suddenly the chance of seeing these shares go through the roof had come along. For a brief moment I'd been lifted out of the gloom that seemed to be dominating my thoughts more and more; it was just the sort of thing I needed to help reverse the trend and maybe change the run of such poor luck I'd been having. Another 'sure thing' turned out to be anything but a good idea. It somehow felt even worse than seeing a horse I'd backed lose, and for me it proved to be the final straw.

CHAPTER FOURTEEN

A COWARD'S WAY OUT

It wasn't long after the shares disaster that I decided to take my own life. What seemed like such a great idea had turned into a catastrophe, to add to a litany of other disasters I was experiencing as a consequence of my gambling.

I realise now how stupid it was to keep things back from John because he was the one working on my behalf to try and get my life back in order. I'd told him about my tax problems, but I hadn't told him I was still gambling or that I owed more money because of it. Once I'd made the decision not to let him in on this other darker side of my life, I found it impossible to come clean, despite the fact that he was not only looking after my affairs, but was also a friend. I suppose I didn't want to lose face. I didn't want him thinking I was a complete idiot. I had respect for him, and I think he had respect for me too. I thought that by telling him everything I might lose that respect.

I knew John and I could work together, and perhaps in the back of my mind I thought that might all come to an end if he knew the full extent to which I was in trouble. So I acted like a coward once more and chose to tell him only part of my problem. I somehow thought that, by not telling him and trying to sort things out myself, everything would eventually turn out okay, but it proved to be an impossible task because I simply wasn't ever able to get ahead of the game. Instead, I had employed my well-worn balancing act – borrowing from one person, using some of the money to keep another creditor sweet, and then betting the rest in the hope that I would be able to get a few quid.

I had become more and more depressed as these efforts failed and really couldn't see any way out of the mess I had got myself into. I was still pretty good at masking my feelings in public, but it all caught up with me once I was back home. I'm sure my mood swings became more noticeable to Jill, Natalie and James. One minute I might be alright, usually because I'd managed to get some money from somewhere, or because I'd had a bet and was dreaming about the horse winning, but then when it all seemed to be going wrong I would just sit there looking glum and acting grumpy. It must have been particularly awkward for the children – they were young and didn't need to have me sitting there in a world of my own looking as if everything was caving in on me. I could also be snappy with Jill and the kids for the most innocuous thing.

I think Jill suspected something was going on but decided to give me time and space to deal with whatever it was. It certainly must have seemed a bit odd at times with me speaking on the phone, often in hushed tones, walking off to other parts of the house so that I could be alone and not overheard. It certainly wasn't a normal existence for her, but she coped with it all and also managed to go off and begin her university degree course in human communication. It must have been very frustrating for her because she could see how down I was and always tried to help when she could. Sometimes she would sit with me and talk about all the positives in my life, reminding me of just how lucky I was in many ways and the fact that I had a lot to look forward to. Quite often we would end the night with me in a much better frame of mind than I had started it, but then in the early hours all the negative thoughts would start to swamp my mind, and by the morning I would feel just as depressed about my life as ever.

If it had just been the problem of the tax I owed to the Inland Revenue, I honestly think I would have coped. All of that was being taken care of and, although I knew that I was going to have to work and wait for it to be sorted out, I had absolute faith in John and all the people working on my testimonial committee. They were some of the best businessmen around and, unlike me, they knew what they were doing when it came to handling money and looking after it wisely. I also enjoyed the involvement I had in the various functions that were planned for me throughout the year. I was a very lucky boy to have people looking after my interests and working towards getting me a clean slate with the authorities, but while all of that was happening I kept my other big problem under lock and key inside my head.

The shares debacle just about summed up the hopelessness of what I was trying to do behind the backs of everyone who cared for me. In my own mind I saw it as an indication of just how bleak things were for me. It didn't really matter that my tax affairs were being sorted out, because I had a whole set of other problems following right behind, and I was simply unable to get a grip on any of them.

I also knew that the everyday matters were being neglected. I dreaded the postman coming every morning because as far as I was concerned he was only going to bring bad news. I used to hate the sound of letters falling on the floor and I used to race to get there before Jill. I didn't want her know the debt I was in or that I wasn't coping with paying bills. I was about eight months behind with the mortgage and 14 months behind on council tax. Everything was such a mess, and I resorted to just taking any letters that were sent to me and stuffing them in an old briefcase. I had gone beyond acting like a normal person and instead had started to retreat further and further away from the reality of my situation. I thought that by ignoring things I would not have to deal with them, and so that's what I did. I pushed it all away, still hoping that a big win or a windfall from somewhere would ease or solve my problems, but the longer it went on the worse it became, and seeing my tip on those shares go so disastrously wrong probably did enough to push me over the edge.

Even with my depression and mood swings, I was still able to hold it all together until that horrible Monday afternoon in March 2002. I may have had the dark thoughts about suicide hanging around me for some time, but that's all they had been, although I'm sure that for a number of years I had seen it as a definite option. That was how crazy some of my thinking had become, but perhaps before that day there was always something within me that said I would find a way out, that I would be able to get hold of some money no matter what and have enough to stave off the problem for a while. Finally, though, I felt as if I'd run out of options.

I was obviously past the point of thinking logically. As I climbed the stairs to my bedroom, all I wanted was a way out. I wasn't ending my life for any honourable reason, or to help anyone else. I was doing it for myself.

I was taking the coward's way out.

CHAPTER FIFTEEN

YOU NEED FRIENDS

After the trauma of my failed suicide bid I knew that getting back to anything like normality was not going to be easy. I did feel as if a weight had been lifted from my shoulders, because now I couldn't hide from what I had tried to do. My closest family and friends were well aware of what I'd done, even if the outside world weren't. There may have been a few whispers behind my back, but they were nothing more than that, and the statement that I had put out after my stay in hospital went a long way to making sure my visit became a non-story.

My main problem was coming to terms with all the pain and hurt I had caused. As well as knowing I had made a mess of my life in so many ways, I now had to carry the guilt I felt for my actions, and I did feel terribly guilty.

Although I said sorry many times to people who I cared a lot about, it still boiled down to one thing: I had committed a selfish act and in the process caused terrible grief and pain to those same people. Some of what I had been covering up was now out in the open. For example, John and Jill had opened the briefcase full of post and found all the unpaid bills that I'd stuffed in there. He quickly began to deal with it all, but shouldn't have had to do that. It had been my responsibility and I had walked away from it, just as I had walked away from my responsibility as a husband, father and a son.

The depression I had felt about my money problems soon became replaced by another kind of depression. This time it was caused by a feeling of low self-esteem. I knew I had let so many people down and yet they had all be so accepting of what had happened. They might have been scared and upset as well, but all they seemed to want to do was help me. It was lovely to have that kind of affection directed towards you, but at the same time it made me very emotional.

I also continued to feel very unsure of myself, which was why I think I was so clingy towards Jill. I could cope when I was out and about doing things like golf days and generally meeting people, but coming home at night or being alone in the house was often very difficult for me and I felt distinctly uncomfortable without her. Jill was incredibly understanding throughout all of this, and I'm sure she must have been wondering if I would try and do something stupid again. I know she always wanted to know where I was and if I was feeling alright. For quite some time she'd had to live with someone who almost had a split personality. She was never certain which kind of man was going to come through the door, and I'm sure Jill and the children must have felt as if they were walking on eggshells sometimes because of the way I had acted towards them. I didn't want to be that way anymore and, having failed to kill myself, I knew I had been given a second chance to try and put things right.

One of the best things to happen to me in the aftermath was getting married to Jill. I had never thought about getting married again, but somehow the whole idea seemed right and it was lovely for me to know that after all I'd put her through she was still prepared to have me as her husband. It wasn't a lavish ceremony, but it was a wonderful day, with our close family and friends all there to see us tie the knot.

I have to confess that, despite enjoying the day and all that went with it, I didn't actually feel very well. I still had my moments of depression, but I had begun to learn to deal with them and I also had the constant support of Jill to help me through when I did feel a bit low. I felt very fragile mentally following the suicide attempt and continued to for quite a few months, but at least those closest to me knew about my emotional state and were prepared to help me cope with trying to rebuild my life.

I was also well aware that I had to try and get to some normality into my everyday existence. I wanted to work and, because of the sort of work I did, I believe it began to help me a lot. I liked interacting with people, I was good at it and it took my mind off things, but I'd be lying if I said that from the moment I realised I'd failed in my suicide bid my life changed for the better. Lots of things in it did, but the fact that I'd survived didn't suddenly mean all my troubles had disappeared because they hadn't. Doing what I did probably helped me to unburden some of the emotions

I felt, and I had to own up to having buried my head in the sand when it came to taking care of things like domestic bills and mundane matters like allowing the post to build up over a series of months without opening it. However, there was still something which remained a secret from everyone close to me, and that was the full extent of debts caused by my gambling.

When I tried to take my own life I was still having a bet, not to the extent I had in past years, but I was still gambling. It was relatively controlled due mainly to the fact that I didn't have the large amounts to gamble as I might have had in the past. I had always been able to get my hands on a bit of money here or there in order to keep the ball rolling, but suddenly I couldn't do that. It had been an uphill battle to keep everything going for some time, but I suddenly found myself climbing a hill that was just too big for me, and I think that's when I snapped and did what I did.

I had told John that I wasn't gambling, but I suspect he realised I still was. Once I came out of hospital and began to get back to a normal kind of life, he'd taken control of my affairs and made sure all the bills were paid on time. He knew the sort of money I was making from things like hosting dinners, golf days, MC and television work, because they were all arranged through the company he was now head of, Champions UK. When we first agreed to work together I'd spent a lot of time at his house as he outlined the sort of role I would have in the future and the kind of work I could be expected to be involved in. I think John was trying to let me know there was life after snooker, and the plan was to start to raise my profile so that I stayed marketable and in the public eye. I liked the idea of working with him and of what the company was going to do. There was genuinely a lot for me to look forward to, but what he didn't realise was that the problems I had created for myself in the past were always capable of pulling me back.

John might have known about my 'official' debt to the Revenue, but he had no idea about my 'unofficial' debt to some money lenders. These debts had built up over a period of time when I was desperate to get my hands on some cash, not only to pay off existing debts, but also to give me some cash to gamble with. By now my total debts were in the region of £100,000. It's a terrible thing to have to admit now, but I still felt, even after trying to take my own life, I could go out and get money by having a bet, despite all the harsh lessons I'd learnt over the years. It was that old gambler's instinct. Once the prospect of getting your hands on some cash comes along, you tend to just go for it. The thought of what it might bring gives you a huge boost, and produces a burst of optimism, that is, until it all goes wrong and you're worse off than ever.

I had resorted to my usual regime of robbing Peter to pay Paul, and that in turn led me to going down the route of using money lenders. It is not something I would recommend.

It's all very matter of fact when you do meet them. I was never asked to go to a deserted piece of ground or a hotel room. It was more a chat in the street or a pub, normal places. It was all very amicable, but I was left in no doubt that it would be stupid to mess them around. These guys never overtly threatened me, but they didn't need to.

"Look Willie, you can have your money, but this is the interest you're going to be paying and this is the date you're going to pay us back," was the sort of thing I'd be told.

At the time I felt I had no other choice. I'd pretty much exhausted every avenue I knew and I had to try to get rid of the debts I had. The people I borrowed money from charged something like £200 for every £1,000 I'd borrowed each month. The interest payments soon mounted up and it was not long before I found myself in a lot of bother. It also meant that I began to heap more pressure on myself as I tried to make sure I got the juggling act right and paid people off when I had to. I don't really know what I was thinking at the time, but I probably saw it all as a quick fix, a way of getting my hands on money that I needed urgently, but as usual I hadn't really thought the whole thing through. If I had done, I would have realised I was only creating more problems for myself, problems which would continue for years after I had tried to kill myself.

The ridiculous thing was that in April 2003 I was given a clean bill of health by the Inland Revenue. Although not all of the outstanding amount was paid back, they got the £100,000 they had been promised. Much of the rest was made up of penalty clauses I'd incurred for not paying money owed on time, and in the end John was able to do a deal with the authorities allowing me to start afresh, without having the dark cloud of possible bankruptcy hanging over me. It was a wonderful feeling to know that I no longer had my tax problems to worry about, but despite all he had done for me and the fact that I would see John on a regular basis and was part of so much of what

Champions were doing, I just could not bring myself to tell him the whole truth about the extent of my other debts. The one he knew nothing about.

I was a bit like a duck in the water. On the surface I looked pretty calm but underneath I was paddling furiously. I used to constantly think about how I was going to get myself out of trouble as payment deadlines approached. I sailed very close to the wind on some occasions. If money was due to someone on 1st February and it was late January, that person became my main concern, but once he'd been taken care of I might have to borrow from someone else knowing that I had to pay another money lender on 1st March, and obviously being late wasn't an option.

It never got to the stage where I was an hour away from getting filled in, and they might never have done that sort of thing anyway, but as I was borrowing money from certain types of people I suppose at the back of my mind I knew that sort of thing could be a possibility.

A knock at the door or a phone call usually did it for me; I would start to wonder if some money was due that I'd overlooked, or there was some sort of problem. It would be wrong to say that I thought all of the money lenders just cared about their money, though. In fact one of the people I had borrowed from came to my house after the suicide bid having heard through the grapevine about what might have happened and sympathised with me. "I didn't realise it was that bad for you," he said as he stood in the doorway.

For more than three years after my suicide attempt I pretty much carried on doing what I had done in the 10 years before it happened. It wasn't as big as it had been before in terms of the money I used and the money I therefore owed. In the past I might have needed to find £50,000 one month to pay off gambling debt, whereas after I'd tried to kill myself I perhaps had to find £1,000 or £2,000, but it was just as difficult to get myself clear.

Instead of going to John again for help or telling Jill about my problems, I decided the best thing I could do was carry on living one day at a time, in the hope that something would eventually turn up and give me enough money to rid myself of yet more financial problems which I had allowed to build up. I couldn't face having to tell John and jeopardise not only a personal friendship, but also a business relationship which was working well for both of us, and I just couldn't stand the thought of worrying Jill after all that I'd already put her through. I decided I just had to try and cope with the situation. I still got depressed, but I think that is part of my character and something which I have learned to live with, even to this day, and there were no more suicide attempts.

Money wasn't suddenly going to drop from the sky to take care of my debts, I had to get on with the work I did for Champions and hope that my juggling act continued to take care of the money I owed. It was a strange existence for me really, and I suppose I had a bit of a split personality. I could be sitting at home with my head in my hands worrying about money and getting depressed at the mess I was in, and then I could be involved in a corporate event, like a dinner or golf day, and switch to being the happy-go-lucky sort of person most people thought I was all of the time. I genuinely enjoyed the work.

Over a period of time through some of the various things I had become involved with on a corporate level, I had got to know one particular guy who was a very successful and wealthy businessman. I'd met him a few times at different functions and he had once invited Jill and I to his house for a lovely dinner which we both really enjoyed. One day I was playing golf with him and we were making small talk when he asked me how I was doing. I'd had a terrible time of it trying to pay one debt and as a result added to another and for some reason I just felt I had to tell somebody.

"If you really want to know I'm doing terrible," I told him.

I think he was quite surprised because he'd only really seen one side of what was happening and what my life was about at the time. When I told him the full extent of my troubles and how much I owed to various people I think he was quite shocked, and I suppose I felt ashamed at the way I had allowed myself to get into so much trouble, but at least I'd told him the truth and come clean about what I had done. What happened next stunned me.

"Willie I'll lend you £100,000 so that you can get your-self straight, but before I do it I want you to tell John Hayes," he insisted.

Although he didn't know John personally, he knew of him, and he was obviously aware of the link I had with him and the fact that we were friends. I think he was surprised that John had been kept in the dark about all of my problems, and if he was going to give me this huge loan he thought it was only right and proper that I should finally come clean to John. Once the offer had been made I felt a huge surge of relief run through my body. The money would take care of all the debts I owed and take a huge weight off my shoulders. For once it really did look as though there would be a fairy-tale ending, but after the initial feeling of relief came another emotion. I began to feel embarrassed at the thought of having to tell John. I worried about what he would think of me and how he would react to being told that his friend and the person he had helped out for the past six years had been keeping a huge secret from him.

My businessman friend insisted that I phone John and tell him that we would be coming to his house to see him. Even when I did this I tried to mask the real reason for our visit and just said I had someone with me who wanted to meet and talk about a possible bit of business. We arranged a time and date to meet without me giving John any more information and a day or two later I arrived in a chauffeur-driven car with the man who was going to help change my life.

We went into John's house and made small talk for about 20 minutes, with me feeling distinctly awkward and ill at ease. I'm sure John thought it was very odd because having brought this man to his house I hadn't made any attempt to explain why we were there. He kept telling John that I had something to say to him, but I would change the subject and skirt around what I was actually there to tell him. I really struggled with it until my benefactor decided I'd put the moment off for long enough and insisted I tell John the whole story. I knew there was nowhere for me to hide and I had to tell John everything – all about my gambling, borrowings from money lenders and just how much debt I was in. When John heard that I was going to be given the opportunity to get out of the hole I was in with this massive amount of money I think he was as surprised as I was.

John has since told me that before he got into his car to leave, my businessman friend stopped and spoke to him.

"I don't know why I've done this," he told John. "I love Willie, he's a great guy, but I know I'll never see that £100,000 again."

"You will," insisted John, and within six months I had managed to repay the loan in full.

I told John where the money needed to go and he sorted it out for me. With the money lenders off my back, John helped me find a way to pay back the guy who had been so generous towards me. I remortgaged my house, worked as hard and as often as I could, and managed to pay off the £100,000 loan. It was an incredible feeling to finally be free of the money worries that I had carried with me for so long.

It was also a huge relief not to have to hide anything from Jill anymore. She was no fool and I now know that she suspected all was not well. She could see the depression in my eyes at times, and hearing the whispered phone calls I made had done nothing to ease her concerns.

Paying off all that I owed left me feeling happier than I had been for years, but at the same time I was also embarrassed. I knew I had not been truthful with Jill or with John. He had been prepared to put his neck on the line and had helped me to carve out a career after snooker. I knew I had done my bit by introducing many of my celebrity friends to Champions, but if it hadn't been for him I would never have become involved in the whole sports and events management business in the first place. Once again I felt as though I had let people down, but having finally rid myself of so many debts I was determined I wouldn't do it again. I wanted to make sure I didn't mess things up again.

Gambling had always been at the root of all of my financial problems. If I had never placed a bet in my life I know how differently things would have worked out. I had terrible regrets about what had happened in the past, but there was nothing more I could do about that. I had to concentrate on the future and make sure I didn't screw things up yet again.

CHAPTER SIXTEEN

STRICTLY
SPEAKING

I n 2006, I was desperate to go into the jungle. Not because I had people chasing me for money again and I needed to get as far away from them as possible, but because *I'm A Celebrity. . . Get Me Out of Here!* was the sort of reality television show I thought I would really enjoy taking part in. Since packing in playing snooker for a living, my profile had gradually been building again. I was lucky in that my television work as a commentator had continued after I stopped playing and that meant a lot of people still associated me with the game, and I loved being involved in a sport that had been such a big part of my life ever since I was a kid. I also did all the corporate work and was involved in various celebrity events with the Champions organization, but John Hayes also wanted to make sure I got exposure in other areas.

I had already appeared on programmes like *Bargain Hunt* and *Can't Cook, Won't Cook,* which were a bit of fun, but probably the two biggest celebrity reality shows then, and now, were *I'm A Celebrity. . .Get Me Out Of Here!* and *Strictly Come Dancing*. I liked both of them but I wasn't that keen on dancing and knew I wasn't very good at it, so it was the jungle experience that appealed to me most. I genuinely thought I would be good on the programme and at the same time enjoy all that went on, including doing the trials that viewers seem to enjoy so much. The people who make the programme were made aware that I'd be interested in taking part in the show and I was invited along to have a chat about the possibility, but nothing more came of it. I was later told that I was first reserve to appear in the event one of the celebrities they'd asked to do it dropped out.

Having got that close, I thought there might be a chance of me taking part in 2007, but that same year Champions were contacted about the possibility of me appearing on *Strictly Come Dancing*. My initial reaction to this was that that I didn't want to do it. I just felt it wasn't for me, but John Hayes persuaded me that it could turn out to be a great opportunity for me and something that I might actually enjoy.

"Willie, this is going to change your life," he insisted.

I wasn't at all sure that would be the case, but I did recognise the power of the programme and how popular it had become during the four previous series which had been broadcast since the show started in 2004. I agreed to go down to London for an interview during the summer of that year with a very relaxed attitude about the whole thing. It would be nice to do the show, but if it didn't happen I wasn't going to be desperately unhappy, and I still harboured hopes that I'd get a call from the *I'm A Celebrity* people.

The interview for *Strictly* went well, and I liked the people I met. I knew I was probably one of many potential contestants they were seeing, but they said they would let me know soon one way or the other. The show was due to be broadcast from the end of September, and that meant anyone who was going to take part would have to start training for five weeks before they actually did their first dance. Within a matter of weeks they called to say I was in, they wanted me to be one of the contestants on the show, which was great but what I didn't realise was how hush-hush the next part of the process was going to be.

I was given a code name, and told that on no account was I to tell anyone that I would be taking part in the show until the full list of contestants was officially revealed. So whenever I was referred to I was known as 'Mr Leicester'. I wasn't even allowed to tell my own mother. It was like being part of the secret service, but once I was in I began to enjoy the whole process.

That year there were 14 celebrities, seven men and seven women, partnered by seven male and female professional dancers. The show had grown and grown in popularity and in doing so had become something most of the nation seemed to be looking forward to by the time the dark nights of autumn came around.

To get started, I went down to London for some publicity shots and to find out who I would be dancing with. I was teamed with Erin Boag, and when she saw me she must have wondered what the hell she'd let herself in for. I'm sure I didn't strike her as a potential winner of the competition, but from the very first day we met each other she was very kind and understanding, as well as being extremely professional when it came to the dancing and training she expected us to do.

After a big press launch where all of us were dressed up in the sort of outfits we'd be wearing on the show, we then had to start thinking about training and making sure precise dates and times were pencilled into our diaries. I think it was probably at that point we all realised just how serious it all was and also how it was going to start to affect all of our lives over the following weeks.

That year the celebrity line-up comprised actors Brian Capron, Stephanie Beacham, Letitia Dean and Matt Di Angelo, model and photographer Penny Lancaster, actress and model Kelly Brook, singer Alesha Dixon, footballer John Barnes, television presenters Dominic Littlewood, Gethin Jones, Kate Garraway and Gabby Logan, along with Gabby's rugby-playing husband Kenny Logan.

I have never had a problem mixing with people, and to be thrown into a situation like that with people I didn't really know was no problem at all. They were a great group of people, and during the course of the show we all got on very well. The problems all came with the training. Don't get me wrong, I enjoyed doing it, but until you actually go and compete in the show you have no real idea just how tough it is. I also became aware very quickly of how good all the professional dancers were. They really knew their stuff, but what was even more impressive was their ability to take complete novices like me and somehow manage to give them the skills and the confidence to go out and dance in front of millions of people who watch the show.

The five weeks of training leading up to the start of the series were hard, but also very rewarding. I suppose that, like so many of the people who take part in the show, I was quite self-conscious about taking my first steps with a partner who was a professional dancer, but Erin could not have been nicer or more supportive. We used to train in Leicester so she would come up on the dates I had available and she'd coach me and put me through my paces. And there was always a cameraman and soundman on hand to record everything said and done. Remember this was going on with the other 13 contestants as well – it was a big operation.

Erin worked really hard to make sure I was ready for my live debut on the show which took place early in October. She is a lot smaller than me, but she was somehow able to move me around and direct what I was doing on the floor. She would put me in the right place to do the steps we'd rehearsed, and even if I made a mistake she'd somehow do the same with her feet and that would cover for me, so there was no great interruption to our routine.

My first dance on the show was going to be a waltz and, although I was nervous to begin with, once I got started the nerves seemed to disappear and I really got into it. It's incredible really, because in training a lot of what I did never seemed to make sense at first, but that's all part of the process and Erin was brilliant at breaking things down. She would give me ten-second segments of dance steps and at first I just wasn't sure it was working, but then you put them all together and the dance is there. It's the best way for someone like me to remember a routine, and when it all comes off it's magical.

Learning to dance and doing the waltz on that first programme was one of the biggest thrills of my life. We danced to a song called *Run to Me*, and I found the whole thing very emotional – even now if I hear it on the radio I start to get a tear in my eye because it brings back so many happy memories. I made a mistake with my steps about ten seconds before the end of our dance but, true professional that she is, Erin went with me and so the whole thing still looked good. . . unless you are an expert, and of course we had four of them sitting beside the dance floor.

The judges are a big part of the programme, and some of their comments get a big reaction from the studio audience on the night. Len Goodman has become a firm favourite as the head judge and he was joined by Arlene Phillips, Bruno Tonioli and Craig Revel Horwood. I have to say that I wasn't too keen on some of the comments made during my time on the show, and a couple of them were quite cutting. I know it was all part of the programme and that's what I signed up for when I agreed to do the show, but at the same time I just thought some of it was a bit over the top. One of the comments I had from Bruno was that I looked like a polar bear in the Sahara, and another comment thrown at me was that I was all over Erin like a Walrus. It just seemed more about getting cheap laughs than adding anything to what I'd tried to do. Len was very different, he would criticise, but at the same time I always felt he was trying to be constructive rather than destructive. I have to admit that I bit my lip when a couple of the comments were tossed my way; after all, I was on live television and I wasn't about to give them a mouthful back even if I felt like doing just that.

My old pal Dennis Taylor had been on the show a couple of years before me and he'd taken a bit of stick for one of his routines, especially from Craig. It must have been a bit too much for Dennis and he told Craig to try and learn to play snooker in three weeks and see how he got on. That was exactly what he tried to do. Someone actually had the idea of doing a piece on Craig learning to play, and guess who acted as his coach? None other than yours truly, so I'd actually met him before and, believe me, he wasn't very good as a snooker player!

When someone like me goes on the show you are like a fish out of water, and sometimes that shows. There's nothing wrong with pointing that out, but it's the way in which it is done which can sometimes make you feel a bit angry. Despite all of this I got on well enough with the judges off camera, and it was a very happy show to be associated with. We all had a giggle doing it and, although I'd made that small mistake near the end of that first dance, I got some reasonable comments from the judges. Len said it was "outstanding", Bruno just mentioned my posture and Craig told me I was remarkably light on my feet. We got a mark of five from Craig and Arlene, while both Len and Bruno gave us seven, making a total of 24 from the four judges, which wasn't a bad start.

We'd been told to try and keep the 12 weeks the show was due to last as free as we could, but obviously people had commitments. In the second week I was involved in a group dance which was a lot of fun and I think we all enjoyed it, not least because I think we all seemed to get on so well and supported each other whenever someone went out onto the floor for their dance. I had wonderful support from everyone and, although it was funny hearing them chanting "Go Willie, go Willie", I also have to say that it meant a lot to me and it showed that in a very short space of time we'd knitted together well. We were all a bit apprehensive at the start of the competition and I think the fact that we all seemed to get on and like each other helped settle everyone down. Quite a few of us would stay at the same hotel on a Friday before the Saturday show and have a rehearsal of our dance. We'd have another rehearsal the next afternoon and then get ready for the real thing that night.

Following the waltz and then the group dance, I was due to dance the tango with Erin, but in the week leading up to it I was in Aberdeen commentating on a snooker tournament, so she had to come up to Scotland and go through all of the moves with me there. It was knackering because we'd be training in the morning, I would be commentating in the afternoon and evening and then it would be back to training the next morning. I enjoyed doing the waltz and was always pretty confident that I'd be alright, but the tango was different. It was hard going. The other thing to remember is that, although you are rehearsing for most of the week for one particular dance, you also have to spend a couple of sessions at the end of the week, preparing for the following week and what you will be dancing if you get through.

I might not have been as confident dancing the tango, but I still thought we would get through on the night. Instead I found myself in the last two places and had to have a dance-off against John Barnes and Nicole Cutler, who had done the jive that night. I actually finished above John in the scoring, but when it came down to the dance-off, judges Craig, Arlene and Bruno all went for John and Nicole. I was out of the show and I was gutted. I'm not going to pretend it didn't matter to me because it did. I was sick about it. I remember appearing on the programme, Strictly – It Takes Two on the Monday after being voted off and crying. I was that emotional about the whole thing, because by that time I had really got into it and realised how much I would miss everyone.

Erin had been absolutely wonderful to me and she is without doubt one of the nicest ladies I have ever met. She had the nickname of 'Miss Whiplash', because she was supposed to be so hard and tough with her partners, but she was always so kind to me and gave me nothing but encouragement. We never once argued and whenever I had doubt in my own ability she would make sure that I snapped out of the mood I was in and began to think positively again. Having thought it was a show I didn't really want to do, I came away from it a real convert. I didn't realise how much fun it could be and how it gets under your skin. For the time I was in it the programme was always in my thoughts and it became such a big part of my life and what I did. That's why it was such a wrench to leave, but I have nothing but great memories and I'm so pleased I did it, because it was such a marvellous experience and totally different to anything I'd ever tried before.

Once I was off the show I avidly kept up with what was going on and who was in and who had gone from the programme. I went down to London a couple of times and sat in the audience as the show was broadcast. The second time I did this I was on crutches after one of the silliest accidents I've ever had in my life. You might have thought the go-cart incident was stupid, but this one probably topped it.

A few weeks after being voted off the programme, I went for a day of golf with some mates. Instead of walking the course we were all going around in buggies, and during the course of playing a hole one of my pals started telling me a story as he drove us towards our golf balls. It was quite a long, drawn-out tale and just as we were slowing down I started to jump out of the buggy without him realising what I was about to do. As I jumped out my leg got caught under the cart and the action of it spun me around. It felt really painful, but we played our shots and then made our way to the next hole. By the time I got there the pain had got worse, so much so that I had to stop playing and head home. Luckily I'd injured my left leg and I had an automatic car, so although I was in pain I could still drive, but as I went down the motorway I began to shake and I knew the injury was probably worse than I thought it had been. I managed to get to the hospital and headed straight for the A&E department. After looking at my leg and taking some x-rays they discovered that I had broken my leg. Just to make matters worse I came out of the hospital on crutches only to find a parking ticket. In my haste to get my leg looked at, I'd parked in a disabled bay.

Having a broken leg was certainly something I could have done without, particularly as I had to carry on working and fulfilling various engagements. It was also very disappointing for another reason because I had been asked to return to *Strictly* for one last time, to take part in their end-of-season show where everyone who had participated in the series was going to do a little routine. I had really been looking forward to it, but with my leg in plaster the whole idea of taking part seemed impossible. The only way it could work was if my plaster and bandages were taken off with enough time for me to have a chance of appearing. I was optimistic my leg would heal in time for me to appear, but about a week before the programme I rang up and said I didn't think I was going to make it. All the people from the show were very understanding, but said that if I could make it I would only have to come on and walk through the whole routine, and that everyone would understand.

I was desperate to go down to London and see everyone again. The show had been such a great buzz for me and I didn't want to miss out on the grand finale. The day before the show I took some painkillers and felt like a teenager. I decided to go down and do the programme and I didn't feel any pain at all. I even started messing around and having a dance at the after-show party and in the end had a great time.

The next morning, I could hardly move and the pain in my left leg was awful. It meant another trip to the hospital where I was told I had rebroken my leg. All the dancing and mucking around I'd done the night before had caused it, but because the painkillers were so strong I just hadn't felt anything. I spent Christmas and the New Year on crutches, and because I was doing nothing but sitting around and eating I put back on the two stones I'd lost during the course of all the training and dancing I'd done for the show.

Despite that painful ending, I still have nothing but happy memories about my overall experience of being on the programme, and I am still an avid viewer whenever it is on. I'm not the only one who has been bitten by the bug. I've since been to plenty of golf days where I've sat at the bar with Dennis Taylor and former England rugby star Matt Dawson, who has also appeared on *Strictly*, and we've done nothing but talk about dancing.

CHAPTER SEVENTEEN

TAKING CONTROL

When I look back on those weeks taking part in *Strictly Come Dancing*, I realise it was more than just being on a television show. It marked a turning point in my life. After all the dark times, I began to move into the light.

My stay on the show might have been relatively brief, but the response I got from it was amazing. So many people recognised me because of my appearance in the series and there is no doubt at all that it had the effect of raising my public profile considerably. From a work point of view that was obviously a good thing, but there was also another side to it. For so many years I had lived with a cloud hanging over me because of my gambling and the debts I'd built up. By the time I did *Strictly* I was clear of all my money worries. I still had to work for a living, but for the first time in about 25 years I felt as if I was finally taking control of my life. I didn't have to keep secrets from my family and close friends anymore, there were no more illicit phone calls or worries about who might be knocking on the door. I had finally put all the bad times behind me and I could start to think about the future.

I allowed gambling to do terrible things with my life and, in turn, I did some terrible things which had an impact on others. I have a mountain of regrets over the way I've messed things up and the hurt I've caused people who were closest to me and who deserved better. I think I was someone who was desperate to do the right thing, but ended up doing the wrong thing most of the time. I have been stupid and cowardly in a lot of my actions and, rightly, I will have to live with the guilt.

That guilt and regret still sweeps over me from time to time, and along with it comes the depression. I still have moments when I am down and feel very low. I have never sought any kind of professional help for this in the form of counselling or psychotherapy. Instead, I have learned to accept that I am prone to periods of depression and because things are so much better for me now than they were in those really dark days, I find I have much more to look forward to and feel optimistic about. When I was burdened by financial worries, depression was never far away. I don't have those kind of problems anymore, but I do have regrets about the way I wasted much of my life. My depressive episodes now are often about what might have been and the fact that had I not been a gambler I could have set myself up for life.

I still think about the money I've wasted throughout my lifetime and what it could mean to me now if I had it. I can't pretend I wouldn't like to have the sort of dough that would allow me to take off to Barbados whenever I felt like it and not worry about the cost, but I don't. What I do have is a wonderful wife, wonderful children, a mother I adore and close friends who are like a second family to me. I have a lovely house, a nice car and a lifestyle that would be the envy of many people. I'm also lucky enough to have the support and goodwill of the general public, something which I am constantly grateful for. The work I do with Champions is something I enjoy very much; it also gives a focus and order to my life. I also like to get involved in charity work with organisations such as Help the Aged among others, and I am a patron of Rainbows Children's Hospice in the East Midlands, all of which has helped to make my life more worthwhile.

I still love snooker and I'm fortunate to be involved with it through my commentary work. It certainly doesn't replace the adrenalin rush I used to get from playing the game and I also used to like having a laugh with the other players, but I certainly don't miss the grinding aspects of being a professional snooker player. While I was a natural player it didn't mean that I could ignore things like having to practise, and sometimes I found that a bit of a slog, but the game itself is something I will always enjoy.

It's great seeing good young players coming through and making a name for themselves, and I only hope they don't make the same sort of mistakes that I did. I have never been the sort of person who likes preaching to others about the way they should live their lives, but I would say to any of the younger players that they should step back sometimes and just think about what they have. All they need to do is devote themselves to the game for ten years, of which probably only five of them will be at the top level.

If I had my time over again I would knuckle down and make sure I made the most of the talent I was given. Hindsight is a wonderful thing and I know that would be my approach now, but when you are younger and have the wonderful feeling that your career will last forever, it is easy to get distracted and do things you shouldn't. My biggest weakness was obviously gambling, but there may be others out there at the moment or who come through in the years to come who like to drink, or go out clubbing when they should be in their hotel room or practising. It is not for me to judge them, but for their own sake I hope they have the common sense that I lacked, and see just what a fortunate position they are in. With Barry Hearn's involvement in the game again, and this time with a controlling interest as chairman of the World Snooker association, there are all sorts of new markets and opportunities opening up for players around the world in places like China and Australia, with the chance to earn very good money. I am not envious of them because I had my time, I just hope that the new generation of players make the most of their careers.

I get to see all the big tournaments, and I think the game is really flourishing again and has a great future. Working at the World Championship in 2011 was fantastic because I think it was the best there has been since 1985 when Dennis Taylor had his epic win in the final against Steve Davis. Having commentated at the Crucible for a number of years, I can tell you that, with all the matches that take place over the 17-day tournament, sooner or later you usually hit a wall where you start to feel a bit fatigued by it all. That didn't happen because there always seemed to be something to look forward to, and of course the performances of Judd Trump got everyone excited.

For the best part of four years Judd's been as good as he is now, but all of a sudden he's found a way of winning. When he got to the final I thought he was destined to win it because of the way he'd played in the rest of the tournament, but he came up against one of the best players of all time in John Higgins. Going into the match I thought that over 35 frames there were going to be six or seven which would be scrappy, and I thought Judd would only be able to win two of those against his more experienced opponent. He nearly pulled it off, though, and losing 18-15 in the way he did shows how well he was playing.

If Judd had won I think he would have been a great champion. He was like a breath of fresh air and everyone liked watching him play. He certainly has the pure ability to go on and become a world champion in the future.

It was great commentating on him and seeing him play exhibition shots. He really entertained the crowd and I don't think I've ever heard an ovation at a snooker match like the one Judd and John got that night before they played their final session.

One man who would have loved to have been watching Judd was my brother, Malcolm, who sadly passed away early the same year, aged 60. He'd devoted a lot of his life to snooker and the amateur game. At one time, he managed the England junior team, and he organised hundreds of tournaments, including many 'One Dayers' at my snooker centre, with up to 128 players taking part. It was really him who ran my club, even if it was my name over the door.

I actually sold the club in 1998 and the money we got for it was split between myself, my mum and my two brothers, but Malcolm continued to take a great interest in snooker and knew all about the young talent that was coming through. He had seen Judd progress over the years, just as he had so many of the other young players who have come through to make a name for themselves.

He had been a bit of a hero to me as we were growing up, and I loved him dearly. He died after battling against cancer, and it did make me question how the world can sometimes be so cruel and also how a life can be taken away so easily. Life is precious, something I am very much aware of now for very good reasons, and that is why I now intend to make the most of mine.

Last year I was given my own little scare when I effectively had a mini stroke. I was hosting an event in London and had invited Jill's son James along to it. I was in the middle of giving a speech when I suddenly felt a bit muddled and confused. I began to stutter and slur my words, but because it all happened so quickly I thought nothing of it. The next day James mentioned what had happened to Jill. In her work as a speech therapist, she had come across the sort of things he described and was aware that stroke victims have similar symptoms. Sure enough, a checkup revealed that I'd suffered a mini-stroke. I suppose it was a warning and I was lucky enough to be able do something about it. My short-term memory isn't as good since, but having changed things like my diet I am more aware of what I should and shouldn't be doing. I might have wanted to kill myself once upon a time, but that is all behind me now. I have a lot to live for and I want to stay fit and healthy.

My old gambling ways are also behind me. I still have the occasional flutter, but it is nothing compared to what I used to do. I still regularly buy lottery tickets in the hope of cracking that big one, just like millions of others and would love to have the sort of money that would allow me to do what I like, when I like, but that just isn't the case.

Perhaps I had to hit the depths I did to realise that I needed to get my act together. I was addicted to gambling, and my rehabilitation has been a slow process. As with my depression issues, I never sought professional help or advice for the gambling problem I had. For me, the change came when the secret life I was leading was finally fully exposed, and I was able to come clean, which in turn lifted a weight off of my shoulders and gave me a chance to re-evaluate my life. I stopped lying to myself in the way I had done. I owned up to what I was, to what I had become, and to the fact that I could never allow myself to wander down that destructive path again.

It's almost as if I have been drip-fed the good sense to finally pull myself away from the habit which caused me so much anguish, and so many problems, for such a big part of my life. I may have been mentally weak at times during my snooker career, but somehow I did manage to find the sort of mental strength I needed to rid myself of the gambling demons that once ruled my life. I no longer have the inclination to go out and try to gamble in the way I once did, and although it has taken a long time I can honestly say that I hate the sort of gambling I was once involved in. The memory of it all and the pain it caused is a constant reminder to me of how close I came to ending up in the gutter.

I could not have pulled myself out of the mire without the love and support of my family and close friends. Apart from having such good people around me, my lifestyle now means that I am able to concentrate on family and work without distractions. John Hayes looks after all my personal affairs, with every penny coming in and going out accounted for. I know that bills are being paid and the money which I earn is taken care of in the right way. I no longer sit and think about where I should place my next bet. My days are busy and I have a diary which is full of engagements.

I no longer frequent the world I used to and, although someone like Racing Raymond has remained a friend, our days at the track and some of the sort of betting we got involved with are in the distant past. Having the good fortune to meet someone who was willing to loan me £100,000 when I was in so much trouble was incredible. When that sort of thing happens you would be an idiot if you didn't stop to think and take stock of your life. That money and the remodelling of my public profile via Champions, *Strictly Come Dancing* and other media work, have given me another chance. I realised that it could be my last chance and that in itself was a big motivating factor in making sure I sorted myself out and didn't slip back into my bad old ways. I let so many people down and that will not happen again. The penny has finally dropped and I now have a real appreciation of what I need to do with the rest of my life. I am determined to move forward now instead of looking back all the time. I have been given the chance to rebuild my life and I want to take it.

I might not have been a lucky gambler, but I have come to realise that in so many other ways, I am a very, very lucky man.

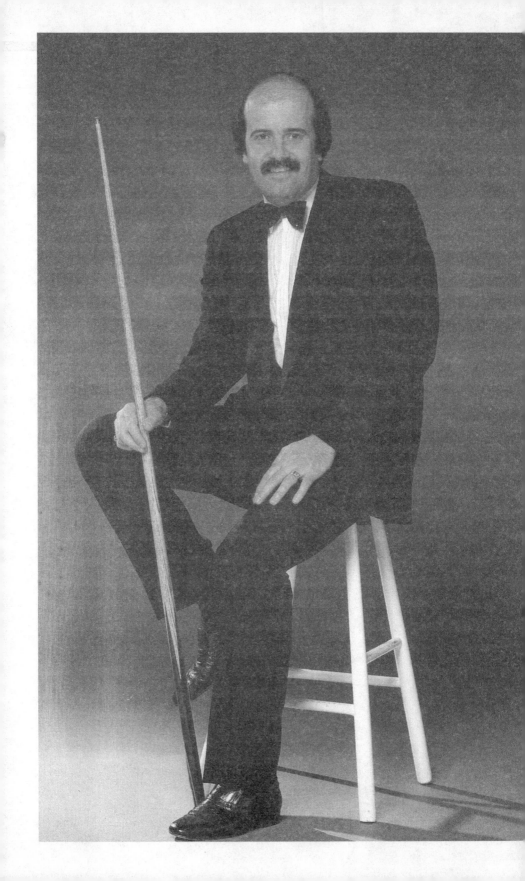